Railroad Company Northern Pacific

Transportation Rules

Northern Pacific System of Railroads

Railroad Company Northern Pacific

Transportation Rules
Northern Pacific System of Railroads

ISBN/EAN: 9783744727938

Printed in Europe, USA, Canada, Australia, Japan

Cover: Foto ©Suzi / pixelio.de

More available books at **www.hansebooks.com**

TRANSPORTATION RULES

NORTHERN PACIFIC

SYSTEM OF RAILROADS.

IN EFFECT SEPT., 1883. REVISED MAY, 1886.

ST. PAUL:
THE PIONEER PRESS CO., PRINTERS.
1886.

GENERAL RULE.

No person connected with the Operating Department of the Northern Pacific Railroad will be permitted to engage in other business, or to be interested directly or indirectly in any industry, the profits of which may be enhanced by facilities which his official position may enable him to afford, or which would occupy time or divert attention from official duties.

The Company requires and expects of every officer and employe entire loyalty to its interests.

The compensation given for services is intended and must be accepted as a full consideration therefor. No employe has a right to expect free transportation for himself or family in addition thereto. Such consideration will only be given in exceptional cases, such as accident, death, or in consequence of other unusual conditions; and it must be positively understood that application will not be made for free transportation for employes of the Northern Pacific Railroad over other roads. Even when sent on business of the Company, it is preferable to pay fare and have the same refunded.

If any emergency arises requiring passes over other roads the application must be made through the office of the General Manager or Assistants, and properly recorded.

GENERAL INSTRUCTIONS.

SECTION FIRST.

1. All persons entering and in the employ of the Company must devote themselves exclusively to its service, attending during the prescribed hours of the day or night, and residing wherever they may be required. **Devotion to service. Reside where required.**

2. They must promptly obey all instructions they receive from persons placed in authority over them, and conform to all the Regulations of the Company. **Obey promptly.**

3. They will be liable to immediate dismissal for disobedience of orders, negligence or incompetency. **Immediate dismissal**

4. To use the credit of the Company is forbidden to anyone, unless special authority is given by the General Manager. **Credit of Company forbidden.**

5. Unless appointed so to do, they are not to receive money on any occasion, or under any pretense whatever, from any person on the Company's account. **Must not receive money for the Company.**

6. All persons in places of trust in the service of the Company must report any misconduct or negligence affecting the interests or safety of the road which may come within their knowledge; and withholding any such information, to the detriment of the Company's interest, will be con- **Report misconduct and negligence.**

sidered a proof of neglect and indifference on their part.

Liable for negligence.

7. All persons will be held legally liable for injury occasioned to persons or property by their misconduct or negligence, and the Company reserves the right to withhold any pay then or thereafter due, to defray the expenses of the same.

Unnecessary work on Sabbath. Whistle as little as possible.

8. No unnecessary work must be performed on the Sabbath; trains in passing through villages on Sunday will use the steam whistle as little as possible.

Persons in apparent ill health.

9. Persons in apparent ill health, and unable at all times to perform the duties to be assigned them will not be employed by the Company. All persons who are authorized to employ men will be held responsible for the strict observance of this rule, and, in case of doubt as to the physical condition of the applicant, the matter must be referred to the Managers or Surgeon of the Northern Pacific Beneficial Association.

Deliver up property in your care.

10. All persons when leaving the Company's service, or at any time when demanded by proper authority, must deliver up the property of the Company intrusted to their care, Whenever property is transferred from one department or officer to another, a receipt specifying the articles must be taken in the prescribed form.

Take receipt.

Penalty for misuse of property.

11. If any of such property shall have been improperly used or damaged, a deduction from pay due shall be made, sufficient to make good the damage, or to supply new articles.

Profane and boisterous language.

12. Persons in the employ of this company having control of men must never, under any circumstances whatever, curse them; boisterous, pro-

fane or vulgar language is strictly forbidden. Civil, gentlemanly deportment is required of all persons employed by the Company in their intercourse with passengers, with the public and with each other. Any violation of this rule must be reported to the Head of the Department under whom the offending party may be employed.

Be civil with each other and the public.

13. All employes of this Company are strictly forbidden from entering into altercation with any other person, no matter what provocation may have been given. They will make a note of the facts if necessary, and report to their immediate superior. Rudeness or incivility on the part of any employe, whatever may be his rank, will meet with immediate punishment.

Altercation, rudeness and incivility.

14. It is required of every employe to be civil and courteous to all with whom he may come in contact; to answer inquiries properly, and to aid passengers and others doing business with the road, in every reasonable manner.

Answer inquiries. Aid transaction of business.

15. The use of intoxicating liquors by the employes of this Company is strictly forbidden, and will be considered good cause for dismissal from the service.

Intoxicating liquors.

16. No employe, whatever may be his rank, will be allowed to absent himself from his duty, without permission from the Head of the Department under whom he may be employed.

Absence without permission.

17. The pay of every man absent or suspended from duty will be stopped.

Pay stopped.

18. The regular compensation of officers and employes covers all risks or liabilities to accidents. If an employe is disabled by sickness, or any other cause, the right to claim salary or pay is not rec-

Compensation covers all risks or liability to accident.

ognized. Allowances, when made in such cases, will be as a gratuity, justified by the circumstances of the case and the previous good conduct of the party, and must have the approval of the Head of the Department where the claim originates.

Observe instructions on printed forms.

19. All officers and employes must carry out the instructions contained in the printed notes on the blanks for reports, which they are required to make to the general and other officers.

Prevent injury to persons or property. Take the safe side.

20. All employes are required to exercise the greatest care and watchfulness to prevent injury or damage to persons or property, and, in case of doubt, take the safe side.

Shall not be re-employed.

21. When a person is discharged from one Department or Division of the Company's service he shall not be employed in another without the consent of the officer discharging him, or that of the Head of the Department or Division from which he was discharged, subject to the approval or the General or Assistant General Managers.

Who are considered train employes.

22. Agents in charge of the United States mails, Express Messengers, Dining Car Employes, Sleeping Car Conductors and Porters, News Agents, individuals in charge of private cars, and persons in charge of stock, while with the trains of the Northern Pacific Railroad, must consider themselves employes of the Northern Pacific Railroad in all matters connected with the movement and government of trains, and must conform to the directions of the Conductor thereof.

Superintendent's authority.

23. Division Superintendents on their several Divisions have authority, by telegraph or otherwise, to change the movements of trains, from the time specified in the tables, and their orders in all respects must be obeyed, unless such orders conflict with these regulations or the requirements of the Auditor, General Freight, General Passenger and Ticket Agents, Car Accountant, Telegraph management, or Engine and Car repairs.

24. In all cases where instructions are not understood, or where the course to be pursued admits of any doubt, the parties in charge shall so act as in no way to compromise the safety or interests of the road, **seeking at the first opportunity, the necessary explanations from the proper officers.**

When instructions are not understood.

CAUTION AS TO PERSONAL SAFETY.

25. Great care must be exercised by all persons when coupling cars. Inasmuch as the coupling apparatus of cars or engines can not be uniform in style, size or strength, and is liable to be broken, and as from various causes, it is dangerous to expose between the same the hands, arms or persons of those engaged in coupling, all employes are **enjoined,** before coupling cars or engines, to **examine** so as to **know** the kind and condition of the drawheads, drawbars, links and coupling apparatus, and are prohibited from placing in the train any car with a defective coupling, until they have first reported its defective condition to the Yard Master or Conductor. Sufficient time is allowed, and may be taken by employes in all cases, to make the examination required. **Coupling by hand is strictly prohibited. Use for guiding the link, a stick**

Exercise care when coupling.

Report defective cars to Yard Master or Conductor.

Guide the link with stick or pin. **or pin.** Each person having to make couplings is **required** to provide a proper implement for the purpose, as above specified. All persons entering into or remaining in the service of the Company are warned that the business is hazardous, and that in accepting or retaining employment they must assume the ordinary risks attending it. Each employe is expected and required to look after and be responsible for his own safety, as well as to exercise the utmost caution to avoid injury to his fellows, especially in the switching of cars and in all movements of trains Stepping upon the front and rear of approaching engines, jumping on or off trains or engines moving at a high rate of speed, getting between cars in motion to uncouple them, and all similar imprudencies are dangerous and in violation of duty, **and are strictly prohibited.** Employes are warned that if they commit them, it will be at their own peril and risk. Employes of every rank and grade are required to see for themselves, before using them, that the machinery or tools, which they are expected to use, are in proper condition for the service required, and if not, to put them in proper condition, or see that they are so put before using them. **All will be held responsible** accordingly.

Hazardous business.

Responsible for safety.

Jumping on or off engines or cars, or going between same.

Machinery or tools in proper condition.

26. Yard men, Train men and other employes are directed to communicate with the Superintendent of the Division, if they are aware of any defects in the construction of the yard tracks whereby an accident might happen while the men are in the discharge of their duties.

Defects in the track.

27. Engineers are directed to exercise great

care in handling their engines, while Yard men or others are making couplings, and must pay particular attention to signals. Conductors and Yard men are directed to report to the Superintendent of the Division any Engineer who fails to obey this order.

Handle engines carefully. Pay attention to signals.

CLEARING THE MAIN TRACK.

28. No wood, timber, or freight of any kind must be piled within six feet of the main track. No building of any description will be allowed within six feet of the main track, nor nearer than four feet of any side track.

Location of material or buildings.

29. Clearance posts will be set between the side track and the main track, and trains on side track must stand inside of this clearance post or protect themselves the same as though standing on main track. Agents and Conductors will be held responsible for cars left standing outside of clearance posts.

Clearance posts.

SECTION SECOND.

SIGNALS.

Definition of Color.

Red.

30. Red signifies Danger.

Green.

Green signifies Train Orders, and has the same meaning as Red when displayed at Telegraph Stations.

White.

White Signals will be used at Flag Stations to Flag Trains for Passengers or Freight, and to denote special or wild trains and light engines, as per Rule 34.

Blue.

Blue Signals will be used at Division and District Terminals by Car Inspectors, also by work trains, as per Rule No. 35½.

Flag Signals.

Red signal or any object violently waved.

31. A Red Flag by day, a Red Light at night, a Lantern swung across the track, a Torpedo exploded thereon, or any object violently waved on the track is a signal of danger, on perceiving which the Engineer shall immediately stop his train, **and will not proceed until he has received information as to the cause of the signal from the Flagman.**

Red signal in center of track; at side of track.

32. A stationary Red Flag or Red Light in the center of track is Signal that track is impassable, and train must be brought to a stop as soon as possible. If train is unable to stop and passes over signal, it will be the Conductor's duty to replace it. A Red Flag or Red Light at the side of track is a signal of caution, and the speed of train must be reduced.

Red signals in front of engine.

Absence of Red signal.

33. Two Red Flags by day, two Red Lights and two Red Flags at night, shall be carried on the front of the engine to indicate that the engine or train is to be followed by another engine or train. The absence of a Red Signal at points where such a signal is usually shown will be considered a signal of danger, and trains must be brought to a full stop and the cause of the absence of such signal ascertained, and the train will not proceed until the way is known to be clear.

White signals in front of engine.

34. Two White Flags by day, two White Lights and two White Flags at night, shall be carried on the front of the engine to indicate that it is an irregular or wild train, but it must be distinctly understood that the White Signals confer **no rights whatever** other than those of an irregular train; and it must be further understood that White Signals, carried on wild or irregular trains, running between two sections of regular trains does not in any way interfere with the rights of regular trains.

A white flag between sections of a regular train.

If an emergency arises whereby two flags or two lights, as required by Rules 33 and 34, cannot be obtained, one flag and one light will indicate the same. It will be the duty of Division Superintendents to require an explanation whenever two lights or two flags cannot be obtained.

When two flags and two lights cannot be obtained.

35. A Green Flag by day, a Green Lantern by night, or the explosion of a Torpedo at Telegraph Stations, indicates that trains are to stop for orders.

Green signals at stations.

35½. A Blue Signal displayed at an appointed place at District and Division terminals indicates that trains are held for inspection or supplies, and must not start until signal is removed.

Trains held for inspection and supplies.

This signal will also be used at the extreme switches of Car Repair Tracks and no engines or trains must enter same or disturb the cars thereon without the sanction of the Car Foreman.

Location of Car repairs.

It will also be used to indicate the location of Work Trains when laid up for the night.

Location of Work trains.

Whistle Signals.

36. Signals by Whistles will be given as follows:

One blast is notice to apply the brakes. **Apply brakes.**

Two blasts is notice to let go the brakes. **Release brakes.**

Three blasts is notice to back the engine or train. **Back up.**

Road Crossings. One long and two short blasts, when the train is running, is a signal for road crossings.

Acknowledge being flagged. Two short blasts when running is notice that the train is about to stop at a Flag Station, or an acknowledgment of being flagged.

*Train has parted. One long and one short blast of the Whistle, repeated at short intervals, is a signal that the train has parted.

Look to side lights. Two long and two short blasts is signal to Conductor to display side or top lights on caboose, which must be acknowledged by the conductor displaying the go ahead signal.

Notify Conductor about work trains. Three blasts when running, given soon as blue light is seen after sounding station whistle, will be notice to Conductor of the location of a work train. See Rule 74.

Call in flagman. Four blasts is notice to call in a Flagman.

See my signals. Five blasts is notice to observe red signals carried by engine.

Call in trailing engine. In snow gangs, five blasts of the whistle is a notice for trailing or assisting engine to move forward.

Train needs assistance. Six blasts repeated at intervals is notice to Track men and others that the train needs assistance and all employes within hearing must repair at once to the engine or train and render such aid as is in their power.

Cattle on track. A succession of short, rapid blasts is the alarm for cattle.

Whistle for station. The length of time required for Passenger Trains to whistle for stations is four seconds, and for Freight Trains six seconds.

Whistle when approaching curves, etc. Engineers on Work or Irregular Trains will sound the whistle when approaching curves or obscure track.

Engine Bell Signals.

37. The signal for starting an engine or train will be given by ringing the bell of the engine, not less than ten seconds before starting. This must always be done before starting an engine. The engine bell must also be rung when approaching Road Crossings, and continued until engine is fully over crossing. Engine Bell.

Signals by Bell or Air Signal Cord.

38. If Air Signal is not in working order, Bell Cords must be used on all Passenger Trains, and must be connected with the Alarm Bell of the engine, and extend through or over the whole train to the rear end of the last car. See Rule 212. Bell cord on Passenger Trains.

One blast of the Air Whistle or tap of the Alarm Bell when the engine is standing is a signal to start. Signal to start.

One blast of the Air Whistle or tap of the Alarm Bell when the engine is running is a signal to stop. Signal to stop.

One blast of the Air Whistle or tap of the Alarm Bell when the engine is running, given immediately after the whistle has been sounded for a station, is a signal to stop at that station. The Engineer will answer by two sharp blasts of the whistle, showing the signal is understood. Flag Station Signal.

Three blasts of the Air Whistle or three taps of the Alarm Bell is a signal to back the Train. Back the train.

Lantern Signals.

39. To Stop, swing a Lantern across the track.

To Back, raise and lower a Lantern perpendicularly.

To Go Ahead, swing a Lantern over the head.

Head Lamps and Rear Signals.

Head lights.

40. Headlights on Engines must always be burning when running after dark, and when passing through tunnels with, **or without,** a Train.

Rear signals.

41. All Night Passenger Trains must carry two Red Lights on rear car, and all Night Freights two or more Red Lights on Caboose. Day Freight Trains two Red Flags. Engines when running alone at night will carry two Red Lamps on rear of tender. Rear Lights should be looked to frequently to prevent them going out.

Instructions Concerning Signals.

When flagged.

42. Engineers, when flagged, will give two low blasts of the whistle as notice that the signal is seen, provided it is not necessary to call for brakes the instant he sees the signal.

Call attention to and respond to signals.

43. Engineers when carrying Red Signals, as per Rule 33, will invariably call the attention of the Engineer and Conductor of opposing trains, wherever met, to his signals by five (5) short blasts of the whistle, which must be answered by two (2) low whistles as an acknowledgment that the signal is heard and understood. When the response is not given, the train giving the signal must **stop** and give notice, and whenever compelled to stop for this acknowledgment, the facts must be reported to the Superintendent. Engineers will also give notice of their signals to Section men and Bridge men by five (5) short blasts of the whistle. When trains being met also have signals, they will answer by two short blasts and then call attention to their own signals by five (5) short blasts, which will be answered by the opposing train by two (2) short blasts.

44. **It must be distinctly understood, however, that the train being passed is not relieved from responsibility** for not noticing the signal on the passing train, even though they fail to hear the five blasts of the whistle, **or if the opposing train fails to stop for the acknowledgment.**

Not relieved from noticing signals.

45. Regular Trains when carrying Red Signals and running in advance of time, will continue the Red Signals. It is understood that Regular Trains in advance of time have only the rights of Irregular or Wild Trains while ahead of time, and when they fail to keep ahead of time they assume all the rights of the Regular Train which they represent. Regular Trains not carrying Red Signals and receiving an order to run in advance of time, **will not** carry White Signals while ahead of time.

Regular trains when flagging will continue signal if run ahead of time.

Regular trains in advance of time will not carry white signals.

45½. Engineers of Freight Trains running after dark will call for signal from the Conductor at every Station where Side or Top Lights of Caboose cannot be seen. Failing to receive this signal they will assume that the train has parted and be governed by Rule 106. See Rule 36.

When Conductor does not respond to whistle for side lights.

46. Every Conductor, Engineer, Train Hand, Station Agent, Telegraph Operator, Track Foreman, Switchman, Watchman, or other employe of the Company, having to make signals, is required to provide himself with signals, keep them on hand, in good order and always in readiness for immediate use. All necessary materials for mak-

Provide yourself with signals.

ing signals—such as Red and White Lanterns, Red and White Flags and Torpedoes—must be carried in the Baggage car or Caboose of every train.

What flagging means.

47. Flagging against trains means a man ahead of the train three-fourths (¾) of a mile with Danger Signals. Those giving signals must locate themselves so as to be plainly seen, and make them in such a manner as to be readily understood. The utmost care must be exercised by train men to avoid taking the wrong signal when two or more trains are passing each other at stations or in yards. Unless both the Conductor and Engineer are positive that the signal given is for them tney will not move their trains until communication is made by word of mouth.

Avoid taking the wrong switching signal.

SECTION THIRD.

STANDARD TIME.

Standard time.

48. The clock in the Dispatcher's office of each Division is the Standard of Time for such Division, and watches of all Conductors, Engineers and other employes of the respective divisions must be regulated daily by this standard. **No excuse will be taken for variation of watches.** The time will be regulated by telegraph from Dispatcher's office of each Division at 12 o'clock M. daily The Standard of Time for all Divisions and Branches east of Mandan is **"Central" or 90th Meridian Time;** for all Divisions and Branches west of and including Mandan to Heron, **"Mountain" or 105th Meridian Time,** and for all Divisions and Branches west of and including Heron, **"Pacific" or 120th Meridian Time.**

Variation of watches.

How regulated.

Compare time.

49. Conductors and Engineers will compare

their watches with the clocks at the points where their runs commence, and will furnish the time to other employes on the road.

BULLETINS.

49½. Bulletins will be kept at all Registering Stations. Additions to Bulletins must invariably be timed, and when they affect trains on line before same can reach a Terminal or Registering Station, must be telegraphed to them and their acknowledgment taken.

SECTION FOURTH.

RULES FOR THE RUNNING OF TRAINS.

50. The **Trains** are **Classed** as to priority of right to the road as indicated on the Time Tables. Classification of trains.

For the purpose of this book, trains will be referred to as "Superior" and "Inferior" Class Trains. Superior Class Trains are First Class Trains; Inferior Class Trains are Second and Third Class. If necessary to refer to Second and Third Class separately, the class in question will be specified.

51. Trains which have their time at stations specified in Time Table are **Regular Trains.** All other trains are **Irregular.** What are regular and what are irregular trains.

52. Whenever a train becomes twenty-four hours (24) or more behind its own time, **it loses all right of track,** and can only proceed as an **Irregular** Train, as per Rule 71. When a train is twenty-four (24) hours late.

52½. All train orders received, excepting such as pertain to abandonments, expire when trains become **twenty-four** (24) **hours** late. Duration of train orders.

Running orders given to Wild or Irregular Trains remain in force until executed or countermanded.

53. **On all Divisions and Branches of the Road, the Eastward and Southward Bound**

Trains shall have the right to the Road against all **Westward and Northward Bound Trains,** of the same or Inferior Class; but no **Eastward** or **Southward Bound Train** must leave any Station or meeting point where by the Time Table it should meet a train of the same class, **until five minutes** after its own time per table, and this five minutes allowed for variation of watches must be observed at every succeeding station until it shall have met the expected train. This rule is not intended to give any rights to a train of an Inferior Class against a train of a Superior Class, but is only to affect the trains of the same class in regard to each other. No portion of the five minutes allowed for variation of watches must be used by trains running in either direction.

Rights of trains.

Direction of branch trains.

54. The direction in which trains, on all branches and operated lines, are considered running, will be indicated on the time card.

Inferior keep out of the way of Superior trains.

55. All trains of an **Inferior Class** must keep out of the way of all trains of a Superior Class going in either direction.

Inferior ahead of Superior trains.

56. Trains of an **Inferior Class** moving in the same direction with trains of a Superior Class, must get out of their way by going on to the nearest siding. On Mountain Districts **an Inferior Train,** ascending, will not precede a Superior Train, without orders, unless it has ample time to reach the top and report before a Superior train is due to leave the last telegraph station at the foot of mountain.

Must not leave ahead of time.

57. A Train must not leave a Station under any circumstances, before its time as specified in the Time Table without a Special Order from the

Superintendent. When no arriving time is specified, Passenger Trains may arrive at stations three (3) minutes, and Freight ten (10) minutes (or less, as may be sufficient for the purpose) ahead of their leaving time, in order to do station business and leave on time, or let following sections come in; provided they do not exceed the maximum speed prescribed in Rule 59. **Passengers may arrive three and freights ten minutes ahead of time.**

58. The running time of a train is intended to be used in running, and not wasted at stations. Trains having slow speed will not wait at stations to kill time, but will consume all the time in running, except as provided in Rule 57. **Do not kill time at stations.**

59. The maximum Rate of Speed for Passenger Trains is one and a half (1½) minutes to the mile. Stock and Mixed Trains three (3) minutes to the mile. Freight and Wild Trains four (4) minutes to the mile, except as provided in Rule 199. See Speed Table, Page 76. **Maximum speed.**

60. Passenger Trains meeting Passenger Trains, whether by Time Table Regulations or by Special Order, will come to a **full stop** between switches and as near to each other as practicable. Passenger Trains will approach all stations with care, and will not pass the first switch at stations where trains of any class are being met, without train being under perfect control. The rate of speed of all trains over switches shall be fixed by Division Superintendents on their several Divisions. **Passenger trains meeting each other.** **Speed over switches.**

61. Inferior Class, Wild and Working Trains will come to a full stop at stations when meeting any train. This rule is hereby modified so as to **Inferior trains stop when meeting any train.**

Stock trains when meeting Inferior, Wild or Work trains.

permit Stock Trains meeting Inferior, Wild or Working Trains, to pass stations at ten (10) miles per hour; providing such Stock Trains learn positively what trains are in waiting, and communicate definitely what trains they (the stock) are. Conductors of Inferior, Wild or Working Trains, having orders to meet Stock Trains, must be on the look out and ready to exchange registers with them. See Rule 62.

Conductors of Inferior trains be on lookout for Stock trains.

62. When trains meet by Special Order or Time Table Regulations the Conductors and Engineers **must inform each other** what train they are; which shall be known as exchange of register. This must be done **by word of mouth, and not by any signal of the hand or fingers.**

Inform each other what you are.

63. **No Train shall proceed** towards a station where it expects to meet a train of the same class having a right to the road **unless** it has **ample time** to arrive at that station strictly at or before the Time Table Time for the latter train to leave that station.

Be sure you have ample time to make meeting point.

64. **No Inferior Class Train must leave a station** immediately preceding a station where a Superior Class Train is expected to be met, unless it shall be able to arrive at the latter station by its average rate of running, and get on siding entirely out of the way of the Superior Class Train, ten (10) minutes before the time the Superior Class Train is due to leave that station.

Inferior must clear Superior class trains ten minutes.

65. No Inferior Class Train shall leave a station immediately preceding a station where they are to be overtaken by a Superior Class Train, unless they have ample time to arrive at the station and get out of their way ten (10) minutes before the Superior Class Train is due to arrive. See Rule 56.

Departing time.

66. Leaving Time of trains is always to be taken for **Card Time.** When a train has but one time at a station such time will be considered as the **Departing Time.**

Fullfaced figures.

67. The **Full Faced** Figures on the Time Tables indicate the regular Meeting and Passing places for trains.

When a Superior class train occupies main track.

68. Should it become necessary for a **Superior Class Train to occupy the Main Track** at a station or turnout, on the time of any train of the same class which by the Time Table should either stop, meet or pass any Superior Class Train at such station or turnout, no signal shall be given to such approaching train except as provided in Rule 70.

An Inferior class train occupying main track on time of a Superior class train.

69. Should an Inferior Class Train be compelled to occupy the Main Track on the time of any Superior Class Train, the Conductor of the Inferior Class Train **must send out the proper Danger Signals to prevent accident.** If Inferior Class Trains are obliged to keep the Main Track at any time when meeting Superior Class Trains **a man must always be sent out with Red Signals** to warn the approaching train, and the Conductor of the Inferior Class Train **must see that the Switches are right** for the Superior Train to go on the siding.

An Inferior class train meeting same within yard limits.

70. When an Inferior Class Train is occupying the Main Track inside of the Yard Limits at stations where Yard Limit Posts are erected, or between Switches at other stations, where by the Time Table a train of its own class should stop, meet or pass any train, **no Signal will be sent out** except where the view is obstructed, or when the weather is such as to prevent seeing far enough ahead to avoid accident, in which case both trains are **alike responsible, in case of collision. Third Class Trains** must protect themselves against **Second Class Trains** in the same manner that Second and Third do against **First Class Trains.**

Special Passenger, Freight, Work trains and Engines, and rights of same.

71. Irregular Trains **shall not be run without an order direct from the Division Superintendent.** They shall be known and described according to their character as **"Special," Passenger, Freight, or Working Trains, or "Special Engines."** Such Trains **have no rights on the road** other than those conferred in the Special Orders by which they run, and, except in cases when they are given special rights over Regular Trains **they must clear the Main Track at least fifteen (15) minutes before Superior Trains and ten (10) minutes before Inferior Trains are due.** See rule 52½.

When an Irregular train quits the use of road.

72. On the arrival of an Irregular Train at its appointed destination, or on its quitting the use of the road when authorized to run back and forth, the Conductor (or Engineer in case of a special Engine without Conductor) shall notify the Division Superintendent to that effect in writing (which must be sent by telegraph and then placed on file by the sending Operator), **and all its rights to run shall then expire.**

Work trains must ascertain position of other trains before going to work.

73. Conductors and Engineers of Wood, Work, and Construction Trains, **must,** before going to their work in the morning, ascertain the position of all trains, and learn positively that all trains due, or for which signals have been carried during the night, have arrived or passed. They shall report to the Division Superintendent where they intend to run and work, and receive a Special Order to do so. All such trains when leaving a station for their work or returning, **must proceed with the utmost caution, and never risk the safety of the road.** They must never be on the road within fifteen (15) minutes of the time that any First or Second Class Train is due. They may continue their work, when of pressing importance, until Third Class Trains approach, **provided a Flagman is kept three-quarters of a mile** (in the direction the train is approaching) with the proper Signals, when they must run before the Third Class Train to the nearest siding. The Flagman in all such cases, must exhibit the prescribed Red Signal, and also, on arriving at his post, must at once place a torpedo on the rail and keep it there until called in by the whistle of his train, or until he is certain his Signal is observed and acknowledged by the Engineer of the Third Class Train. See Rules 36 and 42. **Should he hear the Third Class Train coming after he has been called in, he will remain at his post and flag the approaching train.** Work Trains will not occupy the main track between 8 P. M. and 5.30 A. M. without special orders.

Must report where they are going to work and get orders

Always proceed with caution.

Clear first and second class trains fifteen minutes.

May work until third class trains arrive.

Duty of Flagman on work trains.

Work trains must not occupy main track.

74. Work Trains laying up at night will display a Blue Signal (see rule 35½) at a conspicuous point where it can be seen by approaching trains from either direction. This Signal shall be notice for all passing trains to leave with Watchman of Work Train a regular time ticket. Form 608.

Display a Blue Light.

75. If a subsequent order be given, moving a Work Train beyond, or curtailing the length

Changing the limits of work trains.

of the limits first prescribed for it, **their previous working orders must be recalled.**

Responsible for rear end collisions.

76. The responsibility for Rear End Collisions at Fuel or Water Stations, as a rule, rests with the following train; but if the view is not clear or the weather stormy or foggy, then both trains are equally responsible; provided, however, that an Inferior Class Train will protect itself against a Superior Class Train at Fuel and Water Stations, the same as at other points. In case a stop is made **between stations** for Fuel or Water, the rear end must be protected as per Rule 95.

Trains must not move backward without a man on rear car.

77. No Train will move backward over any part of the road, whether it be on Main Track or Siding, or however short a distance, unless there is a man on the rear end of the rear car before the train is signaled to move backward, who will remain in that position while the train is moving. This will apply to backing trains on side tracks at intermediate stations or in any of the various yards. When making up trains in yards it may not always be practicable to have a man on rear of train. In such cases there must be a man on the ground in full view, to warn persons of danger.

Trains entitled to main track.

Take siding when time can be saved.

Take siding at nearest end.

Always flag if compelled to back in.

78. The Trains possessing the right to the Road are entitled to the Main Track at meeting points, but will promptly take the Side Track when it is known that trains are to be met or passed, and time can be saved by so doing. When practicable trains will always take the Side Track from the nearest end. If from any cause it is necessary for trains intending to take Side Track to run by and back in, a man must be sent with a flag at least one-half mile in advance of the train. Trains should always approach sidings with caution, in anticipation of a train backing in at the near end of the switch.

Approach sidings with care.

79. Trains may consist of one or several sections. When more than one section, the engine of each section except the last shall carry the prescribed signals to indicate that another train is following. See Rule 33.

When trains are in sections.

80. When one section of a train follows another that is carrying Signals for it, the section of train following **has all the Time Table rights of the leading train, and no more.**

Rights of trains being flagged.

81. Whenever one train is to follow another on the same time (which must never occur ascending mountain grades), notice must be given to the forward train, and the Conductor thereof must notify in person all Conductors whom he may meet at stations where he stops of the fact, besides carrying the proper signal. One train following another must be kept at least one mile behind except at stations or water tanks, which must be approached with great care. See Rules 56 and 76.

When one train is following another notify Conductors what you are flagging.

Keep one mile apart.

82. When any section of a train is unable to make the specified time, the Conductor will drop a man with Danger Signals to warn the following train. It is the duty of the Conductor of every train, when the train stops from any cause, to immediately protect the rear end of his train as per Rule 95. No understanding with the Conductor of the following train will relieve you of this duty.

Always protect the rear end of train.

83. Any train following a Red Signal must be run with caution at all stations, on all curves

Follow Red Signals with the greatest care.

and obscure points on the road, on the supposition that the signals have not been everywhere noticed.

Sections of passenger trains fifteen minutes apart.

Light engines ahead of passenger, and freight sections ten minutes apart.

Responsibility of a collision.

Extra precautions in fog or darkness.

84. When two or more Sections of a Passenger Train are run they must be kept fifteen (15) minutes apart. When a light engine is run as first section of a Passenger Train, or when two or more sections other than Passenger Trains are run they must be kept ten (10) minutes apart, except at meeting points, which must be approached with great care. At such points the responsibility of a collision rests with the following train. The following train must approach all stations with great care, expecting to find the leading train at the station. In case of fog, darkness, or at dangerous places, the forward train, as an extra precaution, will send out a Flagman, but it must be distinctly understood that this does not relieve the following train from the responsibility for a collision.

NOTE.—This rule is hereby modified so as to permit a passenger train following a snow plow to proceed as per rule 143.

Engines when running alone carry Red Signals.

85. Engines running alone or in company with other engines or trains must carry Red Signals on the rear of their tenders by night as provided in Rule 41. Such engines must also carry the proper Signals to be used in case of detention or "breaking down."

When Engineers are considered Conductors.

86. Whenever a Train or Engine is run over any portion of the road without a Conductor, the Engineer will be regarded both as Conductor and Engineer, and will act accordingly. He will be required to make the Conductor's running reports and return them to the proper officers.

87. Should one train be held by another between Telegraph Stations, the Conductor of the train thus detained may require the first train passing him bound in the same direction to carry Signals for him to the next Telegraph Station, where he must report for orders, but a Passenger Train shall not carry Signals for a Freight Train when another Passenger Train is to be met at the Telegraph Station or some station intermediate, nor in any case unless the Freight Train is ready to follow immediately.

When a train is held by another between telegraph stations.

Passenger must not flag freight.

88. If it is not possible to let the Regular Train pass without delay, the Delayed Train can, after examining the orders of the train whose rights they are to take, carry the Signals and run ahead of the Regular Train to the next Telegraph Station, where they will notify the Superintendent of the Division what they have done. Should the Delayed Train carry the Signals and run ahead and on the time of a Regular Train, they **must be very particular to notify all trains they meet until they arrive at the Telegraph Station.** If, upon arrival at the Telegraph Station, they receive orders from the Superintendent to proceed ahead of the Regular Train on whose time they have been running, they will notify all trains they meet until their arrival at a station where a Register Book is kept, when they will register the fact that they carried Signals and run as Train No.—— from ——Station to ——Station.

How a delayed train may carry signals and run as a regular.

Imperative duties when assuming rights of delayed trains.

89. It will be the duty of the Agent and Operator at the station where there is no Register Book, and to which Signals are carried as per Rules 87 and 88, to **flag and notify** all Opposing

Duty of Agents at stations where there s no Register.

Trains of the fact, until the expected train for which the Signals are carried has arrived. The Agent or Operator will also notify the Superintendent of the Division that Train —— or Engine ——carried Signals to his station for Train or Engine No. ——and that he will keep Signal out for Opposing Trains until the expected train arrives. In addition to the above, the Dispatcher will notify all trains.

Duty of Dispatchers concerning trains flagged to a non-registering station.

90. Engines or trains that have orders to carry Signals to stations where there are no Register Books kept will be governed by Rule 88.

When engines or trains carry signals.

91. Except as provided for in Rules 87 and 88, Conductors shall not assume the rights or take the time of another train without special orders from the Superintendent. In case Engineers or Conductors change off before the completion of their trip, they must exchange all unexpired orders they may have, and know that they are fully understood by the parties with whom they are changing. Train Crews will not be permitted to change off without the sanction of the Division Superintendent, and no Engineer, without the permission of the Master Mechanic. In either case, the Train Dispatcher must always be informed so that proper record can be made on train sheet.

Secure special orders to assume train rights.

When crews change off.

92. When an Extra Engine is sent over the road on the time of a Passenger Train, it shall be run as the first section of the Passenger Train when practicable, and carry Signals for it. See Rules 84 and 85.

Extra engines as first section of passenger.

93. No Freight or Work Train shall start to follow a Passenger Train until at least five (5) minutes after its departure, and must then follow with great care, being governed by Rule 84. On Mountain Districts they will not follow First Class Trains descending, under any circumstances, without orders, until such trains are duly reported at next telegraph station. Freight trains must not follow each other in ascending or descending mountain grades. Descending Passenger Trains may follow Freight Trains, as per Rule 84. Ascending Passenger Trains will not leave station at foot of mountain until track is known to be clear. See Rule 56.

Freight or work trains following passenger.

Mountain trains.

94. Trains are never to be pushed by the engine when it can possibly be avoided. In case two or more engines must be used, and if for any reason it is not advisable to couple them together, the train must be divided and a part taken by each engine.

Trains must not be pushed.

95. When an accident occurs or when a train stops on the main track between stations, the Trainmen must instantly take all necessary measures to thoroughly protect it in both directions. The rear Brakeman must immediately go back with Danger Signals not less that nine hundred (900) yards, or the distance of sixteen standing telegraph poles, **whether another train is expected or not.** He must have with him three Torpedoes in addition to the proper Flag or Lanterns; these Torpedoes he will place upon the rail five or six rods apart, the farthest one being, if possible, three-fourths of a mile from the obstruction.

When a train stops on the main track between stations.

96. When a Flagman is sent out to signal any approaching train, he must, if possible, avoid stopping on a curve, or behind any obstruction, en-

Duties of a Flagman.

deavoring to pass beyond the same, should such exist, and reach a position where he can be clearly seen from the approaching train, for at least one-fourth of a mile. **The Conductor must know that his train is fully protected in both directions,** and he will be held responsible, if any accident occurs from want of any precaution that could have been taken.

Conductors responsible for proper flagging.

97. When a Flagman is called in and there is not a clear view for one-half of a mile in the rear of the train, Torpedoes will be left on the track.

Leave torpedoes on track if view is not clear.

98. In cases of fog, storm or darkness, the use of Torpedoes is particularly required. Flagmen will, if possible, stop approaching trains before they explode the Torpedoes, and, when they succeed in so doing, will preserve the same for future use. When fog or storm prevents an Engineer from seeing clearly, the crossing signal must be sounded at intervals of a minute until the train is clear of the fog or storm. Trains following a flag during foggy or stormy weather must reduce speed to eight (8) miles per hour, and at each station the Conductor of each section will leave a written notice for the following train, giving the time of departure and warning them about the speed.

Use torpedoes when flagging in fog or storm.

Save torpedoes when not exploded.

Duty of Engineers and conductors following trains in fog and storm.

99. Trains are to be run under the direction of the Conductor, except when such directions conflict with these rules, or involve **risk or hazzard,** in which case the **Engineer will be held equally responsible.**

Trains run under direction of Conductors.

100. Conductors and Engineers are prohibited from making "**Flying Switches.**" The use of sticks when breaking is also prohibited except on mountain grades and when applying the hand

Flying switches and sticks for breaking.

brake on air brake cars, and then only by the approval of the Division Superintendent.

101. Freight Trains that are designated to carry Passengers, must always carry them upon the rear section, when more than one section, except by special order of the Superintendent of the Division.

Freights carry passengers on rear section

102. Trains will not stop at those stations against which an * is placed in the Time Tables, unless it shall be necessary to take fuel or water, meet or get out of the way of trains.

*Trains will not stop.

103. All Trains and all Engines, with or without trains, must come to a full stop at the crossing of all intersecting railroads, at a distance not exceeding 200 feet from the same, and never proceed until the way is known to be clear.

Stop at railroad crossings.

104. In doing work in cities and villages, where, by city ordinance, fines are imposed for blocking crossings, Trainmen are personally liable unless it can be shown that the blocking was unavoidable.

Do not block street crossings.

105. Great care must be taken in handling Stock Trains to prevent injury to stock. Engines taking water must be cut off before reaching the tank, to avoid jerking the stock by getting opposite the tank spout.

Handle stock trains carefully.

When Trains Break in Two.

106. When an Engineer discovers that his train has broken apart, he will give the Trainmen notice by giving two successive blasts of the whistle — the first prolonged, the second much shorter, thus ——— —, and repeat several times

When a train breaks in two or more pieces.

when necessary; and will not stop the forward part until he is sure the rear part is at a standstill. When entirely certain that the rear part has stopped, the forward part may stop, and after sending back a Flag or Signal, will move slowly back to get the detached part of train, but not until a Signal to back up has been received from the rear part of the train, which must not be given unless the rear part is standing still. If the Engineer cannot make sure that the rear part has stopped, he will proceed to the nearest siding, where he will leave the forward part of his train, after which he will Flag his Engine back to the rear part, presuming that it is still in motion, and taking great care not to collide with it. As soon as the men upon the rear portion of the train discover that it has broken apart, they will stop it, and protect the front and rear by the usual Danger Signals. If a following train reaches this detached part before its engine has returned, the following train will not push the detached portion. If any train breaks into more than two (2) parts, the rear part must be stopped first, then the part next forward of it, and so on, using great care not to stop any part so as to permit a following portion to collide with it. When stopped, each portion must be protected by Signals, if possible.

Detached part must not be pushed forward by following train.

Protect each part by signals.

107. To avoid any misunderstanding and unnecessary telegraphing, the following will be observed: Whenever a new Time Card takes effect all trains on the old Card will take the time and rights of corresponding trains on the new Card. If this leaves the new trains ahead of time, they will not proceed without special

When a time card takes effect.

orders until they strike the time of the train whose number they take. If the numbers of trains are changed by change of Card, the trains of the old Card will not take the new numbers without an order from the Superintendent. If the new Card takes effect when certain trains are between stations, all such trains will Flag to the next Telegraph Station. It must be distinctly understood that the moment a new Card takes effect the old one is thrown away, and if the new Card calls for trains that should have left the terminal before the new Card took effect, such trains have an existence from the very moment the Card takes effect, no matter if between stations, and all trains affected will not run against these trains without special orders.

108. Any alteration or modification of these Rules and Regulations will accompany the Time Tables, as Special Instructions; and such Special Instructions will remain in force only while the Time Table to which they are attached continues in use, and will apply only to that Division of the road to which the Time Table on which they are printed belongs.

See time card for modification of Rules.

108½. Every person having to do with track or train service must distinctly understand that no notice will be given of the contemplated running of Irregular trains, and they must be prepared for them at any hour of the day or night.

No notice will be given of Irregular trains.

109. In every case of Doubt take the Safe Side.

In case of doubt.

RESPONSIBILITY FOR THE SAFETY OF SWITCHES.

110. The absolute Rule for the position of all Switches, when not in actual use, is that **they must be set for the Main Track and Locked.**

Switches must be set for main track

Switches must never be left open for another train.

111. A Switch must never be left open for another train or engine, upon the supposition that its Conductor will close it, unless such Conductor assumes its charge. Conductors, Brakemen or others handling switches, must stand by them until relieved, or until switches are closed.

Who are responsible for switches.

112. The Conductor or Engineer who uses a switch is responsible for its position, unless the Switchman or another Conductor or Engineer personally assumes its charge.

Do not move switches if an engine or car is upon them.

113. All persons who are required to open or close switches must never attempt to throw the switch while a locomotive or car is on the **Shifting Rail,** except to prevent an accident.

SECTION FIFTH.

RULES FOR THE RUNNING OF TRAINS BY SPECIAL ORDER.

Each section of a train considered a separate train.

114. In moving Trains by Special Order, **each Section** shall be taken and considered as a **separate and distinct train,** and shall receive and run only under Special Orders addressed to **its own** Conductor and Engineer.

How train orders shall be addressed, written, transmitted, repeated and delivered.

115. All orders for the movement of trains by telegraph will be addressed to the Conductor and Engineer, and written by the Receiving Operator on manifold paper, so arranged that three impressions shall be taken. The Conductor and Engineer addressed shall read the order carefully and, if understood, shall sign it, adding train number, which must be transmitted with it. It will then be repeated back over their signatures to the Dispatcher, who will, if the order is correctly repeated, reply, "Order Number" (give number) "is O. K.," sign and give time, all of which must be recorded on the order, and the whole countersigned by the receiving Operator. One impression of the order, when properly signed, will be given to Conductor, and one to Engineer. The third impression must be kept by the Operator in his manifold book. Receiving Operators **must not, under any circumstances,** repeat an order back until the **personal signatures** of the Conductor and Engineer are first obtained.

115½. Where orders are sent to a train at a non-Telegraph Station through the medium of the Conductor and Engineer of another train, the Conductor and Engineer carrying the order will send back their understanding to the Dispatcher; the order can then be delivered to the other train and have the same force and effect as though signed by them.

Orders sent to trains at non-telegraph stations.

116. All Orders and Messages relative to the movement of trains must be written in full, and no abbreviations used, except the telegraph abbreviations, "12" (How do you understand?) and "13" (I understand.) Figures must be written out in full and duplicated, thus: Twelve thirty (12:30).

All orders must be written in full.

117. A Special Order for the movement of trains, sent by telegraph, **has no force or value,** until the understanding of the Conductor and Engineer has been repeated to the person giving the order, and been approved by him as "O. K.," and not then until the approval is entered upon the order and the Operator has signed his own name thereon. When, by reason of the telegraph failing, or from any other cause the understanding

When special orders have no value.

cannot be sent, or "O. K." given, **the order is void and will be so considered by all concerned.**

Both Conductors and Engineers must sign orders.

118. Both Conductors and Engineers shall sign their names to the order. Neither shall sign for the other, nor the Operator or any other person for either of them, under any pretext whatever.

Both Conductor and Engineer must have copy of order before starting.

119. A Train shall not be started to run by Special Order unless both the Conductor and Engineer have a copy of the order complete as prescribed in Rule 115, in their possession; nor until they have compared the copies of the order, one with the other, and with the understanding given and know that they agree. Operators must not allow a copy of an order to leave their possession until complete, as prescribed in Rule 117, nor enter "O. K." thereon in advance of its receipt, nor sign their names thereon until the order is otherwise all complete.

Operators must hold orders until complete.

Alterations, etc. not allowed.

120. Alterations, Interlineations and Erasures must not appear on orders delivered to Trainmen. Should it be necessary to make any change in first copy, the Dispatcher must repeat the entire order, and a new copy be made by receiving Operator.

Only one person can give orders.

121. Not more than one person on a District or Division shall be permitted, at the same time, to give Special Orders for the movement of trains.

Who may give orders.

122. Division Superintendents and Train Dispatchers under their directions, are the only persons authorized to give such orders, and the authority is limited to their respective Divisions or Districts.

123. Train Dispatchers shall only give orders in the name of the Division Superintendent, adding thereto the initial of their own.

Orders must be given in name of Superintendent.

124. A transfer of the authority to give Special Orders for the movement of trains shall not be made except in writing, containing a specific transfer of the authority, and complete statement of all unexpired orders; and if done by telegraph, an understanding shall be returned before the authority is exercised by another person, and "O. K." given, as provided for Special Orders in Rule 117.

When Train Dispatchers are going off duty.

125. When orders are awaiting the arrival of a train, the Operator must display a Green Signal. On sight of such Signal at a Telegraph Station, Conductors and Engineers **must go at once** to the office to receive and respond to orders. **The Green Signal must invariably be lighted after dark, and in complete readiness for instant use.** Conductors and Engineers must keep a careful watch for this Signal at telegraph stations; and when seen, the train must be brought to a full stop, and they must ascertain from the Operator in charge, the object of the signal. If the orders are not for their train, **they must each obtain a Clearance to that effect,** from the Operator in charge. These clearances must be turned in at the end of each round trip to Dispatcher, and his receipt taken for same on car book.

Display green signal.

Duty of Conductors and Engineers when green signals are displayed.

Green signals must be in readiness.

Keep a sharp lookout for signals. Secure orders or clearance.

Turn in clearances.

126. The absence of a Signal at any telegraph station between the hours of 7 A. M. and 7 P. M., or the showing of a White Signal **at the place where the Train Order Signal is displayed,** is clearance so far as it relates to Train Orders, but

Absence of train order or clearance signals.

at all Night Telegraph Offices (see list on Time Card, changes must be bulletined and wired to trains liable to be affected), between the hours of 7 P. M. and 7 A. M., all trains will consider themselves held for orders unless they receive a clearance, as per Rule 125. In the absence of a White Signal at any night telegraph office, during night, trains must be brought to a full stop and position of Signal Board ascertained before proceeding. Report all such cases to Superintendent.

When a train is held by a 13 order.

127. When a train is held for orders by a "13" order, **they cannot be released by any form of clearance** or notice of bad track or bridges unless the holding order is recalled. **It requires a regular "13" order to release a Train held for orders by a "13" order.**

When an Operator receives an order to hold.

When operators are changing off.

128. When an Operator receives an order to flag and hold a train for orders, the "13" **must not be sent back** until the Dispatcher is notified **"My Signal Displayed."** At change of night and day Operator, the relieving Operator will sign holding orders, and have them repeated to Dispatcher for his O. K.

When giving orders against passenger trains

129. In giving orders against Passenger Trains, Dispatchers will in every case get the understanding from Conductor and Engineer of train having the right to the road, before moving any train against them, except at Terminal Stations, where Dispatchers may depend upon Operator, Green Signal and the signature of two or more responsible employes to the order. The signatures of Agent and Yard Master, with the Operator, are preferable, but, if they cannot be obtained, then the signature of any other responsible employe will answer. If it is not possible to obtain the additional signatures without serious delay, and the train to be held is obliged to pass the telegraph office before it can leave the station, then the Green Signal and the Operator's signature can be used for moving trains against, but the Operator must secure the additional signatures as soon as possible. If, however, the train can pull out of the yard without passing the telegraph office, then **under no circumstances** will trains be moved against it until the three signatures are obtained to the order.

130. The general rule to be observed in moving Freight Trains against each other is to obtain the understanding of the Conductor and Engineer of the train having the right to the road before running any train against them. If, however, the conditions are favorable for holding Freight Trains through the Operator and serious delays can be avoided thereby Dispatcher can depend upon the signature of the Operator, Green Signal and Torpedoes to hold such ruling train for orders at any Telegraph Station, other than the meeting point, and in extreme cases trains can be held for each other at the meeting points by putting out Red Signals and Torpedoes 1,000 feet in both directions from the Telegraph Office in addition to the Green Signal and Torpedoes at the Telegraph Office. When there is no Telegraph Office at the meeting point, the Red Signal and Torpedoes must be used for holding at the Telegraph Office distant from the meeting point.

When moving freight trains against each other.

NOTE.—Dispatchers will understand that in the use of the Torpedo with Green and Red signals, as provided by rule 130, that in each case the order to use the Torpedo must be given by them to the Operator. If any emergency arises whereby the Torpedo should be used in any other case not covered by rule 130, an order must be given by the Dispatcher to the Operator. Any unnecessary use of the Torpedo impairs its value as a signal of danger.

Holding freights at terminals. At Terminal Stations, Freight Trains can be held as provided in Rule 129.

131. Before any Train is moved against an Operator's Green or Red Light, it will be the duty of the Dispatcher to inquire of the Operator the condition of his Signal Lamps and the number of Torpedoes he has on hand, and at seven o'clock each night all night offices will report the condition of Green and Red Lamps, and number of Torpedoes on hand.

Ask the Operator the condition of his signal, etc.

132. Every precaution must be taken to prevent orders from being forgotten, and to this end avoid holding trains beyond too many telegraph stations.

Prevent orders from being forgotten.

132½. Train or Enginemen are positively prohibited from going to meals or delaying their trains for any cause after receiving an order which allows them to proceed, without first obtaining express permission to do so from the Train Dispatcher, and when such permission is received the Conductor must report when he is ready to go and ascertain if any further orders for him.

Getting meals after orders are procured.

133. All Special Orders for the movements of trains will be given in the forms herewith prescribed:

Forms of orders.

Meeting Orders.

FORM A.

Conductor and Engineer Train No...... Do not pass ....until Train No......, Conductor.................. arrives.

FORM B.

Conductor and Engineer Train No.......run to .... regardless of Train No......Conductor ....

NOTE.—The word "regardless" as used in Train orders has the same significance as the word "meet."

FORM BB.

Conductor and Engineer Train No. ...... meet Train No......Conductor..................at..................

If trains are moved against more than one Section the order should read:

Conductor and Engineer Train No......:
Run to..................regardless of First and Second Sections Train No......Conductors..................and ....or First, Second and Third Sections, etc.
Or, meet First, Second and Third Sections Train No...... Conductors..................etc.

Running Ahead Order.

FORM C.

Conductor and Engineer Train No. .... run from ....to..................ahead of Train No......

Upon this form of Order, the slow train will run ahead of the fast train to the point designated, but not ahead of its own Card time, or exceed its maximum rate of speed.

FORM D.

Conductor and Engineer Train No......:
Train No......runs from..................to..................ahead of you. Left..................at.........

Abandoning Order.

FORM E.

All Concerned, or Conductor and Engineer Train No......
Train No....... of this date, April sixteenth (16th), is abandoned on....................Division, or East or West of..................

Carrying Signals.

FORM F.

Conductor and Engineer Train No......:
Carry signals from.................... to.................... for ....Conductor or..................Engineer.

FORM G.

..................and Engineer:
Carry signals for...............Light Engine or.............. Conductor, and run as Second Section Train No......from ....to........... ...

FORM H.

..................and Engineer:
You will run as Third Section Train No ......from ....to..................

Working Order.

FORM I.

..................and Engineer:
Work to-day, April sixteenth (16th), between............... and..................wild (or irregular or special), (or avoiding Regular Trains). Flag against....................Work Train or Extra on same ground or East or West of..................... *He* is not (or is) flagging against you

(NOTE: If it becomes necessary to change the limits of a Work Train during the day, their previous working orders must be recalled)

Irregular, Wild or Special Trains.

FORM J.

Run from.................to.................wild (or special) (or avoiding Regular Trains). Run.........miles per hour. Flag against Jones. (State what kind of a train Jones is running.) East or West of..................... *He* is (or is not) flagging against you.

(Note: The word "Wild," as used in Train Orders, has the same meaning as "avoiding Regular Trains," and the words "Irregular" or "Special" can be used in place of "wild" if desired).

Flagging and Holding.

FORM K.

Agent and Operator:
Flag and hold Train No......at...................for orders.

or

Agent and Operator:
Flag and hold First, Second and Third Sections Train No.......at..................for orders.

The Dispatcher must be absolutely sure the Train has not arrived or passed the station before using this form of order. If the train has arrived or is passing the station this order must not be used. (*See Rules* 129 *and* 130.)

Time Orders.

Orders of this kind should only be given in case of an emergency.

Second Class Trains running ahead of or against First Class Trains, following form of Order will be given the First Class Train:

FORM L.

Train No......will run............minutes behind Schedule Time from..................to..................

Upon this Order, the First Class Train will run not less than ten (10) minutes more behind its Schedule Time than the time specified in the Order.

Following form of Order will be given the Second Class Train:

FORM M.

Train No......can use.........minutes on the time of Train No......to run from................to.................

Upon this Order, the Second Class Train can use the time of the First Class Train as indicated, in order to make the designated or any intermediate station, ahead of, or against the First Class Train, but not ahead of its own Schedule Time.

Running Ahead of Time.

FORM N.

In running Regular Trains in advance of time, if it is intended that the train shall leave the station where the Order is sent, in advance of time, the Order must read:

Leave..................Station, and run to................in advance of time.

If it is not intended to leave that Station in advance of time, the Order must read:

Run from................Station to.................Station, in advance of time.

Double Order.

In using this form of Order, send to all trains affected, at one and at the same time, when it is practicable to do so.

An Order for a Definite Meeting Point.

FORM A B.

Train No......Conductor..................and Train No...... Conductor..................will meet at..................

.Upon an Order of this form, the train arriving first at the station named will wait until the other train arrives, unless the Conductor and Engineer receive another Order authorizing their train to proceed.

An Order giving one Train the Right to the Road against another, to a certain point, until a certain time.

FORM A C.

Train No......Conductor..................
Has or can have until.........to go to..................against
Train No......Conductor..................

Upon this Order, the first-named train has the right to run to the station designated up to the given time, or before, but not ahead of Schedule time, and from there it will be governed by Time Card rules. Should the first-named train fail to reach the station designated within the time allowed, it will run as per Schedule, against the other train. In such case the train last named in the Order will not leave the station designated until **five minutes** after the time allowed for the first-named train to arrive, after which time it will run as per Schedule.

Recall Order.

FORM A D.

Order to meet Train No......Conductor ....
at........................is recalled.

(NOTE.—If more than one Section was to have been met, the Sections must be designated as "First," "Second," "Third," etc.)

To Change Meeting Point.

FORM A E.

Meet Train No .....Conductor ....
at........................instead of..................

(NOTE.—If more than one Section, spell them out, viz.: "First," "Second," "Third," etc., Conductors............................)

This Form to be used when the opposing train has not received its order for a definite meeting point. If, however, the meeting has been definitely contracted for, and the opposing train has received its orders, then the following form will be used:

FORM A F.

Order to meet Train No .....Conductor...... ....
at..................is recalled.
Meet Train No....... Conductor....................................
at............................

In all cases where Special Orders are not fully understood, ask for an explanation, and in every case of doubt **take the safe side.**

SPECIAL INSTRUCTIONS IN RELATION TO DISPATCHING

Particular attention is directed to the various dispatching rules, which must be followed as closely as possible, and whenever an emergency arises which calls for any temporary modification of established rules, all the necessary precautions for absolute safety must be taken. **Observing dispatching rules.**

When in certain emergencies a particular kind of order is necessary, for which no regular form can be furnished, the Chief Dispatcher will supply the form of order to be used. **Chief dispatcher will supply form of order.**

Double Orders must be used to the utmost extent consistent with reasonable promptness in moving trains. **Use double orders.**

Time orders the exception.

Time Orders, except for work train service and for moving slow trains ahead of fast trains, must be the exception and not the rule.

Forms of order prohibited.

Orders reading like the following: "All former Orders recalled;" "Order No. ...... is void or recalled;" "All trains due have passed," must be discontinued.

NOTE.—The words "all trains due have passed" may be used in extreme cases if the Dispatcher has two checks on all trains having passed.

Ask if clearance were given both Conductor and Engineer.

Dispatchers must aid in the observance of Rule 126 by asking Operators frequently if both Conductor and Engineer received the clearance. Rule 126 is an extra **precaution rule and must never be used to move trains against.**

Trains must not be run ahead of time.

Regular trains must not be run ahead of time or faster than the prescribed rate of speed except when there is good and sufficient reasons for so doing.

NOTE.—Superintendents must so far as practicable be kept advised of the necessity for modification of above rule in order that the practice of running trains in advance of time or increasing their speed may be kept at its minimum.

Keep trains apart.

It is the duty of Dispatchers to hold following sections of trains when they are known to be running too close and keep them the prescribed time and distance apart, and in stormy weather the utmost care must be exercised in blocking the sections a safe distance apart.

Trains on mountains.

Dispatchers **will not permit two freights on the Mountains at the same time going in either direction. Freight trains must never follow Passenger trains down Mountains, but Passenger trains may follow Freight trains.** See Rule 84.

Meeting points on mountains.

Meeting points, when it is possible to avoid them, must not be permitted on the Mountains. A Passenger Train can pass an

Inferior Class Train already on the Mountain, but it is better, when possible to avoid even this, and permit only one train at a time on the hill.

Chief Dispatchers or Division Operators must fully examine and instruct all new Operators in the matter of Train Signals and handling of Train Orders, before they are allowed to commence work. If this cannot be done before Operators commence service it must be attended to at the first opportunity.

Examine and instruct new operators.

Division Superintendents will make frequent examination of Train Order Books and hold Dispatchers to a strict accountability for the observance of the forms.

Superintendents examine train order books.

INSTRUCTIONS TO BE OBSERVED IN CLEARING THE TRACK OF SNOW AND ICE.

134. When two or more engines are coupled together, the forward engine will (except in case of danger, when any engine will signal), be considered the Signal Engine, and the direction the forward engine is going will govern all others in the gang.

The Signal Engine in a snow gang.

135. When starting for, or backing out of a snow drift, the forward engineer **will first place his lever in proper position,** and then signal the other engines. The second engineer will answer the signal first given, only when **entirely ready** to give his engine steam. The third engineer will answer the signal of the second engineer only when **entirely ready** to give his engine steam, etc. The last signal given will govern **all engineers** in giving steam to their engines, which must be done on the instant.

Duties when starting for or backing out of a snow drift.

Duty of Engineer on following or assistant of snow gang.

136. In case a following or assistant engine is employed, it will keep at least one-half mile in the rear of snow gang, and be prepared to move forward the instant required. Five blasts of the whistle is a signal for following engine to move forward to assist snow gang, and the signal should be **answered** by the same signal.

When engines become fast in snow bank.

137. In case engines become fast in snow bank it is best to shovel out one of them at a time, and clear the track of snow. The released engine then becomes a helper for the others.

Use judgment when running into snow bank.

Break edge of drift.

Head Engineer acts in absence of Conductor.

138. In running for snow banks, engineers must, in absence of express orders, as regards speed, use their best judgment, considering the condition of track and bank. When snow is badly packed and frozen, the edge of drift should be broken to allow plow to follow under with safety. In absence of an experienced conductor, head engineer will frequently examine snow banks before running, and especially when snow is deep, or badly drifted upon one side of track.

Have full pressure.

139. It is useless to run into snow banks with low steam, and Engineers will therefore pay particular attention to having full boiler pressure before making a run.

Preparations necessary for snow-bucking.

140. On regular Snow-Bucking Expeditions the pilots of pushing engines must be removed, and engines thoroughly equipped with substantial drawheads, firmly bolted. Also an extra supply of links and pins, and the coal in the tender well covered with tarpaulin.

Snow plows as first section of Passenger train.

141. Snow plows running ahead and on time of Passenger Trains will pull beyond the station building and await the arrival of the train before proceeding.

142. Everybody interested must understand that plow engines cannot use headlights, and that the shoe of the plow is liable to crowd torpedoes off the rail without exploding, and the frequent use of the injector in low temperature blinds the Engineer by steam, thus requiring the greatest possible care in flagging plow engines. **Flagging snow plows.**

143. In blizzards, when it is necessary to follow the plow closely, Engineers of following trains will allow as much time as possible between the plow and the following train. All Engineers should mark the bad cuts, and in severe storms every precaution should be taken to ascertain if the plow engine is through the cut or has had time to get a flag back. **Particular attention is called to this rule.** **Caution in blizzards**

144. No man is worth anything in **Snow Plow Gang** who has not perfect confidence in himself, engine and plow. Anyone who does not feel this is requested to inform his superior. **Confidence in self, engine and plow.**

RULES FOR THE USE OF WESTINGHOUSE AIR BRAKES.

145. In making up trains, all couplings must be united so that the brakes will apply throughout the entire train. The cocks in the brake-pipe must be opened (handles pointing down, **|**), except that on the rear of the last car, which must be closed. **When making up trains.**

146. In detaching engines or cars, the slack must always be released before attempting to separate the hooks, and the couplings must

When detaching engines or cars.

invariably be parted by hand. The cocks in the main brake-pipe, behind hose, must always be closed before separating the couplings to prevent application of the brakes.

How to release brakes when engine is not attached.

147. If the brakes are set when the engine is not attached to the train or car, they can be released by opening the release-cock usually put in the end of brake-cylinder. Engines must in all cases have full maximum air pressure before being coupled to train.

Engine must have full air pressure.

Automatic Brake.

Straight Air Brake.

To cut brakes out.

148. For the Automatic Brake the handle of the four-way cock must be turned **horizontally** (▬). If turned down (▮) it will be changed to **Straight Air Brake**, if turned midway (╲) between these two positions it will close communication with the brake-cylinder and reservoir, and should be so turned when desirable to have the **brakes out of use** on any particular car, on account of the breaking of rods, etc. It is very important in order to avoid detentions, to keep the handles of these **Four-way cocks** in their proper positions.

When straight air is desired.

149. If desired to use brake as **Non-Automatic** or **Straight Air,** turn the handles of the **Four-way cocks** down (▮) on all the cars in the train. When Freight trains are only partially equipped with air brakes use **Straight Air (▮).**

Trainmen.

Be positive the brake is connected.

150. After making up or adding to a train, or after a change of engines, the rear Brakeman shall ascertain whether the brake is connected throughout the train.

Hang up hose.

151. When hose couplings are not used for connecting the brakes between two cars, they must be attached to their dummy couplings.

152. When there is occasion to apply the brakes from the cars, the valve must be held open to allow the air to escape until the train is brought to a stand still, but this method of application should **only be used in cases of emergency.** How to apply brakes.

153. Trainmen must in all cases see that the **Hand Brakes are off** before starting. Know that hand brakes are off.

154. Before detaching the engine or any cars, the brakes must be fully released on the whole train. Neglecting this precaution, or setting the brakes by opening a valve or cock when the engine is detached, may cause serious inconvenience in switching. Hand Brakes must always be set on Air Brake cars set out at intermediate stations. Setting brakes when engine is detached. Set hand brakes when freight cars are set out.

Mountain Grades.

155. Before starting up or down grades which exceed one hundred feet per mile and one-half mile in length, examine brakes and air apparatus carefully. Also make a test before starting from any point if engines or cars have been changed. Special attention is called to the "Retaining Valves" which may be set horizontally (▬) on descending grades of over one hundred feet per mile. Conductors will be held responsible for this duty as well as the relieving of the valves at foot of grade. Examine brakes on Mountain Districts. Retaining valves.

CONDUCTORS.

156. All Conductors will be at their trains, at Terminal Stations, thirty minutes in advance of their leaving time per Time Table, and by First duty of Conductors.

their **personal attention** insure leaving promptly on time. (*See Rule* 168).

Responsible for safe management of trains.

157. Conductors will be held responsible for the safe management of their trains and for the strict performance of duty on the part of the men engaged with them. In order to secure effective work, Conductors must make themselves familiar with the duties required from other train employes, and see that they are fully performed.

Be familiar with the duties of other train employes.

158. They will require their Brakemen to assist ladies, children, and infirm persons off and on the cars, and will render such assistance themselves when necessary.

Assist persons from train.

159. Conductors are positively forbidden to send word to another train, either by telegraph or otherwise, that they want the other train to take the siding. If a train whose place it is to take the siding cannot get on the switch, **they must not pass the frog without first stopping and sending forward the prescribed Danger Signals.**

Must not order trains to take siding.

160. Every Conductor will inspect the **Bulletin** before the departure of his train from Terminal Stations, and will compare time with his Engineer. Conductors and Engineers will compare time with other Conductors and Engineers when meeting on the road, if practicable to do so.

Inspect bulletins, compare time.

161. Promptness in doing work at station is enjoined. **Make every minute count.** The running time of a train between stations is intended **to be used in running, no matter how slow it is.** This rule applies not only to freight trains doing work at stations, but also to passenger trains in loading and unloading passengers and baggage. See Rules 57 and 58.

Perform station work promptly.
Consume the time running.

162. If a Conductor discovers anything wrong with the track, bridges or culverts, which would be likely to cause an accident to a following train, **he must not rely wholly** upon the telegraph to notify other trains, but must leave a flagman in addition to telegraphing.

Precaution when the track, bridges or culverts are dangerous.

163. Conductors when notified of a defect in the telegraph ahead, must (unless there is a Telegraph Repairman on the train) station a Brakeman to watch for the same, and when found, report its character and location to the Telegraph Operator at the next office.

Watch closely for defects in telegraph.

164. Conductors must, when practicable, stop their trains to let Telegraph Repairmen off at defects of the above description, or to take them on when necessary to facilitate their movements to repair at other points.

Stop train for telegraph repairer.

165. Whenever an accident occurs which involves the loss of life, serious injury of persons, damage to property, or the obstruction of the road; or whenever the road is found impassable on account of snow, or damage by flood or other cause, the Conductor or person in charge must report the fact to the Division Superintendent or head of the department, by telegraph, as soon as practicable, giving all information necessary to a clear understanding of the case, such as the location, nature of, cause and extent of the injury, damage, or obstruction, and what relief or assistance is required.

Notify Superintendent promptly by wire of accidents causing loss, etc.

166. They must report in writing to their Division Superintendent, at the end of each trip, all accidents that have occurred to the train or in consequence of its running; such as getting off

Report all accidents in writing, at end of each trip.

the track, uncoupling of cars in the train, killing stock, injury to persons or property, either on the train or otherwise, failure in any way of the engines, insufficiency of the supply of fuel or water, defective places in bridges or roadbed, and any other information that may be desirable to communicate. In case of injury of person, or loss of life, or damage to private property, Conductors must take the utmost care to furnish a full and exact statement of all the facts, with the names and addresses of the persons who witnessed the occurrence.

When necessary to "Saw by."

167. In cases where several trains meet at stations where it is necessary to "Saw by," the senior Conductor in the service of the Company, present, will take full charge for that particular occasion, and all interested will obey his orders.

Register.

Do not pass without order or clearance.

Leave time tickets with work train watchman.

168. Conductors must enter in the Train Register Book at all Terminal Stations of Divisions and Districts, or wherever such books are kept, immediately before departing and upon arrival, the time of departure or arrival of their trains, number of engine, name of Engineer, number of cars of each kind in train, and whether signals carried or not, and if taken down at intermediate stations, so note. **No Train must pass a Registering Station without an order or clearance.** (See Rule 126.) Conductors must also leave a report at all night telegraph stations and with work train watchman on the regular form of blank (No. 608), giving arriving and departing time at that station, if signals were carried and for whom.

SPECIAL INSTRUCTIONS TO PASSENGER CONDUCTORS.

169. No Passenger Conductor will permit any employe of his train to smoke while on duty. He will also observe this rule himself.

Must not smoke.

170. In starting a Passenger Train from Division Terminals, **it must always be done with the air signal cord.**

Start Passenger trains with air signal.

171. Should an engine of a passenger train break down on the road, the Conductor has the authority to take any engine that he may meet or overtake.

When a Passenger engine breaks down.

172. Conductors of trains carrying passengers are required to have the names of the stations at which they stop announced twice in each car **distinctly.** If there are no Brakemen on the cars, this duty will devolve upon the Conductor.

Announce stations.

173. Conductors of trains carrying passengers are required to pay particular attention to the lighting, warming and ventilating of the cars, and the supply of water in the tanks. Conductors of trains carrying emigrants will look to their comfort, and give them every opportunity to provide fresh water at water tanks, supplied by wells.

Look to the lighting, warming, ventilating, and supply of water.

174. Passenger trains will be made up in the following order, which must be observed, no matter how inconvenient or troublesome it may be: Freight Cars, if any, next the Engine; then Mail, Express, Baggage (or Baggage and Express as may best suit the service), Emigrant, Smoking, Second-class Coaches, First-class Coaches, Chair, Dining and Sleeping Cars.

Order of making up Passenger trains.

175. Conductors of passenger trains will invariably require their air-brake hose tested, cylinders and connections examined, and engine air

See to air brakes and signal before leaving terminals. signal sounded, if possible, from the rear coach of their train, before leaving each division station. They must inspect, or require some member of their crew to examine, the train at least four times over each division, paying particular attention to journals, and reporting defects, especially in the air brakes, specifying the number of the car or engine on which it occurs.

Have trains examined carefully.

Use hand brakes once each day.

176. At one point on each division, and at one point on each branch line, trains using the air brake will be stopped once daily with the hand brake; The station where this stop is to be made will be designated by the Superintendent.

Look to the printed matter offered for sale.

177. Conductors will look to the printed matter sold on their trains, and see that nothing improper is offered. Should anything improper be offered, they will prevent its repetition, and promptly report the facts to the Superintendent.

News agents.

178. Conductors must not permit a News Agent to enter upon the discharge of his duties unless he has upon his cap the badge designated for him to wear. They are responsible for the good conduct of the News Agent while on duty, and have authority to prohibit his acting in such capacity for that trip, if he has failed to carry out the instructions given him. Every case of insubordination on the part of News Agents must be reported to the Superintendent.

Conductors wear uniform.

179. Conductors of Passenger Trains, when on duty, are required to wear the regulation uniform.

Mail and express must be considered as baggage when transferring trains.

180. In case of an accident, whereby passengers and baggage have to be transferred, Conductors must understand that they are to treat express and mail matter the same as baggage, and will

render all the assistance they can in making such transfer, and must handle all baggage with care, and will be held responsible for unnecessary breakage.

181. When, from any cause, Conductors of passenger trains leave cars at any station without orders, they must notify the Superintendent of the fact by telegraph from the first office, giving the initials, numbers and kind of cars, the siding where left and the reason for leaving them; and such information must be wired to the Car Accountant at St. Paul. They must also look to the **Train Equipment** (see Rule 200 for list) and if seals on Equipment Boxes are found broken, report same to Superintendent and have equipment examined and boxes resealed at first District Terminal.

Report by telegraph, cars set out.

Look to Train Equipment.

SPECIAL INSTRUCTIONS TO FREIGHT CONDUCTORS.

182. In doing work at stations, Conductors are required to carry out the wishes of the Agent in placing cars, etc. If the Agent's orders are unreasonable, the facts can be reported to the Superintendent of the division. **Under no circumstances whatever will the Conductor undertake to settle the matter by dispute.**

Oblige the agent.

Avoid disputes.

183. In doing switching at stations, where you are required to disturb cars that are being loaded or unloaded, you will be particular to leave the cars in the same position as found. **Agents are required to notify the Superintendent of the division of every instance wherein this rule is violated.**

Replace cars disturbed by switching.

184. You are held **personally** responsible for

Personally responsible for the proper care of freight.

the proper care of all freight while in your charge, and you will be careful to see that the same is delivered to the Station Agent according to the manifests. Conductors and trainmen will under all circumstances be careful in handling freight in their charge. A failure on the part of any employe to observe this rule will be deemed a sufficient cause for his discharge from the service of this Company.

When compelled to leave a "bad order" car.

185. When a Freight Car is set out because it is defective and unsafe to run, the Conductor must see that the words "Bad Order" are written conspicuously with chalk on both sides, and the defective part marked with a cross (×); the fact must also be noted on car report.

When cars leave the track.

186. When cars leave the track they must not be turned over, thrown down embankments, broken up, or otherwise damaged, merely to get them out of the way. Every effort must be made by trainmen to put them on the track with as little injury as possible, and to take the damaged cars to a siding. The Conductor will call on Sectionmen, or any other convenient force, for assistance, which must be promptly rendered.

When a load must be left short of destination.

187. If from any cause it becomes necessary to leave a loaded car at any station or side track before reaching its destination, Conductors will leave way-bill with the Agent where the car is set, or if there is no Agent, the way-bill must be left at the next station where there is an Agent, making proper indorsement on bill, why and where the car was left, and report the same at once by telegraph to the Superintendent, giving number and initial of car, with what loaded, destination and why left. If the property is transferred into other cars, check the contents against the way-bill and make proper notation on same and also on the car report. This notation should show the name of station where such transfer is made; the date of transfer, the numbers of cars into which the property is transferred, the seal numbers of both the car from which it was taken and loaded into, also the condition of the freight and the kind of weather while transfer was being made.

When freight is transferred.

188. On loading a shipment at a point at which there is no Freight Agent, Conductors will obtain a shipping bill or shipping order describing the articles, or will make a list of the same which will be handed to the Freight Agent at the first station at which there is an Agent, when a way bill must be made at the rates provided in the Tariff, or by the General Freight Department, from the point where the freight was taken. If the consignment is destined to a point at which there is no Freight Agent, or to which Tariffs or instructions require prepayment the Conductor will collect the charges from consignor at Tariff rates. The shipping order or list together with any cash collected in prepayment of charges must be handed to the Freight Agent at the next station beyond the point of loading. When delivering any cash to Agent in payment of charges the Conductor will obtain Agent's receipt for the amount on his car record book. When freight is offered at a point at which there is no Freight Agent and destined to a point at which there is no Agent, Conductors will make the following notation across the face of the re-

When freight is loaded at flag stations.

When freight is destined to a flag station.

Take agent's receipt for cash payments.

ceipt given for such shipments: "This shipment to be unloaded at......station solely at shipper's risk upon express agreement that the company shall not be held liable for any loss on, or damage to, or for any delay in delivery thereof."

Unloaded at shipper's risk.

In case the owner refuses to agree to this condition the Conductor will decline to receive the freight for delivery at the point at which there is no Agent and issue shipping bill to the regular station nearest to the point to which the freight is destined and note on the way bill, "Notify consignee at........."

When freight is delivered at flag stations.

189. For the delivery of freight going to stations where there are no Agents if consignee is not there to receive it, you must call the attention of Trainmen to the fact and condition of delivery, noting their names as witnesses on way-bill, which must be left as directed in Rule 188.

Consult with Drovers.

190. Conductors of trains carrying Live Stock are required to consult the wishes of the Drovers in matters pertaining to the care and comfort of the Stock, except when such wishes conflict with the rules and regulations of the Road.

Look to the comfort of stock.

191. Conductors having Live Stock in their trains, unaccompanied by a Drover, will render such assistance and care as is necessary for the comfort of such stock.

Comparestock car numbers.

192. When Live Stock is unloaded for transfer and feed, or other purposes, and is reloaded, Conductors will be particular to observe that the car numbers agree with the original bill; or, if they do not agree, that both the original numbers and the numbers of the cars to which the Stock is transferred are noted on the bill. No excuse for failure in this respect will be entertained.

193. Be particular to unload freight at proper destination, and at Junction Points you must know that you have unloaded or switched all freight taking different directions.

Unload freight and set out cars at the proper station.

194. When in charge of Way Freight Trains, Conductors must check, the freight they deliver on the bills in the presence of the Agent, noting on them anything over, short or damaged, and report the same by telegraph to Superintendent, and on their car report.

Check out freight in presence of Agents.

195. You are required to deliver Way Freight at Way Stations on the platform of the freight house, or at such other proper and reasonable places as the Agent may designate. (See Rule 182.) Agents will not fail to report promptly any refusal on the part of Conductors to comply with this regulation.

Unload freight where agents request.

196. After unloading freight from a car containing freight for other stations, Conductors must see that the articles left in the car are not in a position to fall down.

Guard against freight falling in car.

197. Conductors must carefully examine the seals, locks and cleatings of cars, and keep such a record of the condition of the same as will enable them to give clear and definite answers to inquiries. They will inspect, or require some member of their crew to examine, the train at least four times over the division, paying particular attention to journals and brake attachments.

Examine locks and seals.

Have train examined.

198. The Conductor will be held **personally** responsible for the proper care of Speed Records. He must carry the keys, attend **personally** to winding the clock, putting in and taking out of records. Car Inspectors at Terminal Stations will attend to the oiling, but it is the duty of the Conductor to know that it is done, and to report any negligence in this respect. At the end of each Round Trip the Conductor will send his record of speed to Division Superintendent's office, noting delays, etc. Should the Speed Record get out of order on the Road, and the Conductor is unable to put it in order, he will telegraph the fact at once to Division Superintendent. Cabooses must not be cut off trains, or trains cut in two, except at stations and yards where work is to be done, **making it necessary to do so.** Trains must not leave such station or yard until the caboose and whole train are coupled tegether. Any employe, of whatever grade or rank, who may show a dispositiŏn to obstruct the working of the Speed Recorder will be dismissed from the service. Trainmen and others will use their best efforts to facilitate the proper management of Speed Recorders, thus reducing the liability for accidents, thereby insuring greater safety to themselves and the Company's property in their charge.

Speed Recorders.

199. The maximum rate of speed that Freight Trains are allowed to run is eighteen (18) miles per hour when equipped with Speed Recorders in good working order, and when not so equipped the speed must not exceed fifteen (15) miles per hour.

Speed of Freight trains.

200. The following Tools, etc. are designated as equipment for Baggage and Caboose Cars, and Freight Conductors will be required to make out a monthly report of same, noting all deficiencies, how they became so, and if any repairs are required. (See Rule 181.)

Caboose equipment.

One Switch Rope.
Two Chains.
One Jack Screw.
One Pair Wrecking Frogs.
One Packing Iron.
One Packing Hook.
Three Red Flags.
Two Red Bullseyes.
Three White Flags.
One Dope Bucket.
One Water Bucket.
One Can for Lubricating Oil.
One Can for Signal Oil.
One Draw Head complete.
Extra Links and Pins.
Extra Coupling Sticks.

One Train Box, containing—

One Axe.
One Hatchet.
One Hand Saw.
One Monkey Wrench.
Three White Lamps.
Three Red Lamps.
One Doz. Torpedoes.
One-half Doz. Car Brasses.
One-fourth Doz. Wedges.
Half-Doz. Draw Head Keys.

TRAIN BAGGAGE MASTERS.

201. Train Baggage Masters report to, and receive their instructions from, the Superintendent of the division or General Baggage Agent. They

Duty of Train Baggagemen.

are under the immediate charge of the Conductors of their respective trains, and will obey them accordingly, so long as their instructions do not conflict with the rules and regulations of the Company. Train Baggagemen will carefully observe all instructions given them by the General Passenger or Baggage Agent relative to baggage. **They will use the utmost care to secure the correct delivery of same.**

Be at car before train time.

202. They are required to be at their cars at Terminal Stations at least forty-five minutes in advance of Time Table leaving time.

Aid the Conductor.

203. They are expected to aid the Conductor as may be in their power in promoting the safety of their trains, and whenever necessary they will apply the brakes or render such other services as may be required, or the Conductor may direct.

Allow no one to ride in baggage car.

204. Conductors and Baggagemen will allow no Persons to ride in the Baggage Car whose duty does not require them to be there.

Must stay in car.

205. Baggage Masters will ride in the Baggage Cars, and in no other cars in the train.

Wear badge.

206. They will be required to wear the regulation badge while on duty.

Corpse in baggage car.

207. Baggage Masters will receive no corpse for transportation beyond this Company's lines, unless accompanied by a physician's certificate, showing that death was not caused by any contagious disease. They will also require the same certificate, when it is practicable, before transporting a corpse between Local Stations, but in every case they must have positive information that death was not caused by any contagious disease.

208. They will in no case receive for transportation any corpse which may have become perceptibly offensive, even in the slightest degree, whether accompanied by a physician's certificate or not, nor any corpse unless the case or casket is strong and well secured.

Offensive corpse

209. Train and Station Baggage Masters are particularly cautioned against the careless handling of Baggage; **trunks are not to be broken.** Conductors will give sufficient time to receive, transfer or discharge Baggage with proper care, and in case Baggage shall be injured through carelessness of Baggage Master, the Conductor will report the same, with the probable amount of damage, to the Superintendent, that the amount may be deducted from the pay of the Baggage Master.

Handle baggage carefully.

210. Train Baggage Masters must handle and deliver all Mail at proper destination, when no Mail Agent is on trains for that purpose.

Care of mail.

BRAKEMEN.

211. Brakemen are under the orders of the Conductor.

Obey Conductors.

212. Passenger Brakemen must be at the Starting Station **forty-five** minutes before the departure of their trains; examine the air signal, and brakes, look over train, and fasten badges on their caps. If it becomes necessary, on account of the failure of the air signal, to use the continuous bell cord, Brakemen should be careful, when setting out a car, to release the cord at rear of train, first, then draw it through the hood of coach before uncoup-

Be on hand before train time.

Attention to air signal and bell cord.

ling, and knot same outside of hood at both ends, so cord cannot be drawn through car, to the injury of passengers and windows.

Be neat and civil.

213. Neatness in personal appearance, and civility toward passengers is enjoined.

Lamps, heaters, and ventilators.

214. They must have their lamps trimmed and ready for lighting, and see that the heat and ventilation of the cars are properly regulated.

Uniform.

215. Passenger Brakemen, when on duty, are required to wear the regulation uniform.

How to brake.

216. Brakemen will not apply brakes so tightly as to slide a wheel, nor allow a brake to remain applied **over three minutes to the same wheel** while in motion, but in descending grades will use the Brakes of several cars to check and regulate the train, and **change brakes frequently.** On mountain grades the rear Brakeman will, when train is ascending, remain on caboose, take care of rear end, and be ready to stop train in case it breaks in two. When train is descending his position will be in the middle of train.

Location of Brakemen on train.

Study the rules.

217. Brakemen must study these rules and be prepared to take charge of train in case of sickness or absence of the Conductor. They will be required to provide themselves with sticks, which must in all cases be used when making couplings.

Secure sticks for coupling.

218. When a Brakeman is sent out as a Flagman by the Conductor, he shall be held equally responsible with the Conductor for the faithful discharge of the duties set forth in Signal Rules, and should the Conductor be disabled, or for any other cause the order is not given to protect the train by a Flagman, the rear Brakeman must at once proceed to carry out rules whether trains are due or not.

Duty as Flagman.

219. Brakemen or other employes are prohibited from thrusting their heads out of car windows to note the movements of the train. When it is necessary for the Conductor or Rear Brakemen to look ahead, it must be done from the cupola or platform of the car, and they must see that they do not expose any portion of their person sufficiently to be struck by bridges or other obstructions. **Do not expose yourself to danger.**

220. Tail Lights must be taken to the rear of the train without passing through the sleepers, when it is possible to do so. **Do not go through sleeper with rear lights.**

221. Forward Brakemen when riding on the engine will act under the orders of the Engineer in all matters pertaining to the safety of the train. **Head Brakeman obey Engineer.**

ROAD FOREMAN OF MACHINERY.

222. The Road Foreman of Machinery is the representative of the Master Mechanic on the Road, and his instructions relative to the care of engines, loads of engines and use of fuel, and all other matters in the Machinery Department, will be obeyed. **Authority of Traveling Engineers.**

ENGINEERS.

223. Engineers belong in the Department of Motive Power, and in all things relating to that Department, are strictly responsible to the Superintendent of Machinery, or his proper representative; but in all matters connected with **Road Service** or **Train rights and duties,** they will receive their instructions direct from the Superintendent of the Division. **To whom responsible.**

224. They are required to be at their engines, so as to get them out of houses, forty-five minutes in advance of Time Table leaving time, or sooner if necessary.

Be on engines before train time.

225. They are required to inspect the General Bulletin Boards, as well as those in Round Houses, before starting from Terminal Stations.

Inspect bulletins.

226. They will compare time with their Conductors before starting from Terminal Stations. They will also, when practicable, compare time with other Conductors and Engineers whom they may meet on the Road.

Compare time.

227. Each Engineer is held responsible for the engine under his charge, for the general efficiency of the machinery or working parts, the cleanliness of the same, and for the proper working of the air-brake. He must in no case carry excessive pressure of air, sixty pounds being the maximum pressure for from two to six cars, or seventy pounds for seven or more cars. They must report, on arrival at Terminal Stations, any failure of the air-brake, or any defects in the appliances connected therewith, and must know that they are in proper order before leaving such station.

Responsible for engine.

Maximum air pressure.

Report defective brakes.

228. Engineers and Firemen must be careful in the use of all property belonging to the Company, especially Tank Discharge Spouts, which must never, in any case, be pulled over or thrown from the tender while the engine is in motion. The spouts must always be allowed to empty themselves before being thrown off the tender, and they must also see that the spouts are properly secured before leaving.

Handle property with care.

Allow tank spouts to empty.

229. Engineers must not take any wood or coal at other points than those designated by the Proper Officer, except in case of emergency, when they will inform the Superintendent of the Division by telegraph, and the Superintendent of Machinery in writing, of the amount taken and point taken from; if from a car, the number and initial of car must be given.

When they are obliged to take fuel.

230. Engineers will use every precaution to prevent fire catching from their engines along the line They must carefully and frequently inspect nettings or other apparatus provided for averting sparks, and see that they are in good order. They will not throw out any burning waste or similar material along the line.

Prevent fire on line.

231. Engineers must close the dampers of their engines, and use as little steam as possible in **crossing all bridges.**

Close dampers when crossing bridges.

232. Engineers must pay particular attention to the various Signals displayed by Bridgemen, Trackmen and others. When a Danger Signal is shown, **never receive instructions concerning it until you come to a full stop.**

Pay attention to signals.

233. Engineers will not allow any person not employed upon their engines to ride there, except the Officers of the Road, the Conductors of their trains, the Supervisors of Bridges and Track, and as provided in Rule ~~290~~. 298

Must not allow any person to ride on engines.

234. The number of cars assigned as the ordinary loads for engines, is fixed with a view to the general grades of the Road. Between certain points, where the grades are favorable, more can frequently be hauled. Engineers must be governed accordingly, and must co-operate fully

Number of cars per train.

with Conductors in this matter, both striving to advance the interests of the Company.

Report striking persons, etc.

235. Engineers will report without delay to their Conductors, all the facts connected with the striking of any person, animal, wagon or the like, upon or near the track. Also any negligence on the part of their Brakemen.

Make report of accidents to Superintendent.

236. In cases where any injury is done to any Person, or Team, or to any Live Stock, or where property is damaged, the Engineer will make out his own separate report of the facts to the Superintendent of the Division, in addition to the Conductor's report of the same and upon the same form.

Display signals properly.

237. When instructed to carry Signals of any kind, they must display them properly, and see that they continue in proper position and condition throughout the trip, or until taken down in accordance with orders.

Must not whistle when passing a passenger train.

238. Engineers, except to prevent accident, will not sound the whistle when any part of a Passenger Train is passing them.

Who may handle engines.

239. Engineers are forbidden to allow **any person to run or handle their engines,** except he is appointed so to do by the Superintendent of Machinery, Master Mechanic of Division, or Foreman of Engine House. In case of disability of Engineer, the Fireman, if considered competent by the Division Master Mechanic or Foreman, may be authorized to complete the trip in his stead.

Defect in track.

240. When any unusual defect is observed in the Track, the Engineer will stop and examine the cause, and, if unsafe, the Conductor shall notify the Sectionman in charge, and leave a man with proper Signals to warn approaching trains, until the track is repaired.

241. Engineers must protect front end of train by sending the Fireman out as Flagman when no other Flagman is available. When the Engineer cannot see the Signals on side of rear car, he will call for them to be displayed by giving two long and two short blasts of the whistle (see Rule 36), and if Signal is not then displayed, will consider that train has broken in two, and will be governed by Rules 106 and 244.

Protect front of train.

Call for rear signals.

242. Engineers when applying the Air-Brake must not use the full pressure of the air except in cases of emergency. For ordinary stops the air must be applied slowly, and at a sufficient distance from the stopping place to enable them to stop without discomfort to passengers, sliding the wheels, or injury to the machinery or the train.

When applying air brakes.

243. When the Air-Whistle or Gong on Engine is sounded as a Signal to stop at Flag Station the Engineer will answer by two short blasts of the whistle. (See Rule 36.)

When the air whistle or gong is sounded.

244. Engineers or Firemen should look back frequently to see that all is right; and in case the train is broken apart, **great care** must be taken to keep the forward part out of the way of the detached part, and every precaution used to prevent a collision. Engineers will in all cases go back after the detached portion, with their engines under the protection of a flag, but must be absolutely sure that the detached part has stopped. Trains coming up behind will wait indefinitely, unless otherwise ordered by the Superintendent.

Look back frequently.

When train has broken in two.

Following trains must not push detached part.

245. The use of oil is directly under the care of the Engineer, and his duty is to use only what is necessary. The Fireman oils the valves, but he is under the orders of the Engineer doing so; and so with all stores used on engines, the Engineer is the responsible party.

Use of oil.

TOOLS.

246. Engineers must know that their engines are supplied with all proper tools, and extra links and pins, and that they are in good order for use.

Proper tools.

247. LIST OF TOOLS.

One Spanner Wrench for air pump.
One Spanner Wrench for injector checks.
One Spanner Wrench for feed pipes.
One Wrench for rod bolts.
One Wrench for rod set screws.
One Wrench for eccentric straps.
One Wrench for eccentric set screws.
One Wrench for cylinder heads.
One Packing Wrench for piston rods.
One Packing Wrench for valve rods.
Two Wrenches for piston packing.
One Wrench for pedestal brace bolts.
One Wrench for wedge bolts.
One 15-inch Monkey Wrench.
One 12-inch Monkey Wrench.
One Scoop Shovel.
One Coal Pick.
One Ash Hoe.
One Slush Bar.
One Broom.

One Water Bucket.
One Engine Chain.
Two Wrecking Frogs.
One Pinch Bar.
Two Cold Chisels.
Two Engine Jacks, with Levers.
One Small Jack and Lever.
One Hand Hammer.
One Soft Hammer.
One Hand Saw.
One Axe.
One Packing Hook and Iron.
One Torch.
Two White Lights.
Four Red Lights.
One Blue Light.
One Extra Globe for each Signal Color.
Two Red Flags.
Four Torpedoes.
Two One-Quart Oilers.
One Tallow Pot.
One Two-Gallon Tallow Bucket.
One Two-Gallon Engine Oil Can.
One Two-Gallon Valve Oil Can.
One One-Gallon Signal Oil Can.
One One-Gallon Headlight Oil Can.
Six Flue Plugs.
Two Tender Truck Brasses.
One Engine Truck Brass.
Two Wedge Blocks for raising Engine.
One Set Hard-Wood Blocks for guides.
One Ball Cord for guide blocks.
Two Extra Rod Keys.
One Extra Air-Brake Hose (standard length).

One Extra Air-Brake Hose (8 inches longer than standard length).

One Extra Air-Brake Hose, between Engine and Tender.

One Extra Air Signal Hose.

One Extra Water Hose.

Three Extra Links and Pins.

One Extra Headlight Chimney.

Engineers will be required to make out monthly report as above, noting all deficiencies in the list of Tools, and repairs needed to the Tools on hand.

A TABLE—Showing speed of an Engine, when the time of performing Quarter, Half, and One Mile is given.

Speed per Hour.	Time of Performing ¼ Mile.	Time of Performing ½ Mile.	Time of Performing 1 Mile.	Speed per Hour.	Time of Performing ¼ Mile.	Time of Performing ½ Mile.	Time of Performing 1 Mile.
Miles.	M. S.	M. S.	M. S.	Miles.	M. S.	M. S.	M. S.
5	3 0	6 0	12 0	33	0 27	0 54	1 49
6	2 30	5 0	10 0	34	0 26	0 53	1 46
7	2 8	4 17	8 34	35	0 25	0 51	1 43
8	1 52	3 45	7 30	36	0 25	0 50	1 40
9	1 40	3 20	6 40	37	0 24	0 48	1 37
10	1 30	3 0	6 0	38	0 23	0 47	1 34
11	1 21	2 43	5 27	39	0 23	0 46	1 32
12	1 15	2 30	5 0	40	0 22	0 45	1 30
13	1 9	2 18	4 37	41	0 21	0 43	1 27
14	1 4	2 8	4 17	42	0 21	0 42	1 25
15	1 0	2 0	4 0	43	0 20	0 41	1 23
16	0 56	1 52	3 45	44	0 20	0 40	1 21
17	0 52	1 46	3 31	45	0 20	0 40	1 20
18	0 50	1 40	3 20	46	0 19	0 39	1 18
19	0 47	1 34	3 9	47	0 19	0 38	1 16
20	0 45	1 30	3 0	48	0 18	0 37	1 15
21	0 42	1 25	2 51	49	0 18	0 36	1 13
22	0 40	1 21	2 43	50	0 18	0 36	1 12
23	0 39	1 18	2 36	51	0 17	0 35	1 10
24	0 37	1 15	2 30	52	0 17	0 34	1 9
25	0 36	1 12	2 24	53	0 17	0 34	1 7
26	0 34	1 9	2 18	54	0 16	0 33	1 6
27	0 33	1 6	2 13	55	0 16	0 32	1 5
28	0 32	1 4	2 8	56	0 16	0 32	1 4
29	0 31	1 2	2 4	57	0 15	0 31	1 3
30	0 30	1 0	2 0	58	0 15	0 31	1 2
31	0 29	0 58	1 56	59	0 15	0 30	1 1
32	0 28	0 56	1 52	60	0 15	0 30	1 0

FIREMEN.

248. Firemen belong in the Department of Motive Power, and, in all things relating to that department are strictly responsible to, and receive their instructions from, the Superintendent of Machinery, or his proper representative; but in all matters **connected with the road service or train rights and duties,** they will receive their instructions direct from the Superintendent of the Division under whose orders they are at all times subject to, after crossing the turn-table for service.

To whom responsible.

249. While on duty they are subject to the directions of their own Engineers, and will obey their instructions and render them such assistance, in the performance of their duties, as may be practicable.

Obey Engineer.

250. They are required to be at their engines, at starting points, in time to have them out of the house forty-five minutes in advance of Time Table leaving time or sooner if necessary.

Be on hand before train time.

251. In addition to the performance of their regular duties, they will, in cases of emergency, act as Flagmen, as required by Rule 241, or perform such other extra duties as may be necessary to secure safety to trains.

Act as Flagman.

252. They shall, when not engaged with other duties, assist in keeping a constant lookout, and will instantly give their Engineers notice of any obstruction that they may perceive, or of any signals observed from their trains; or, in case they shall have reason to believe their trains have parted, they will immediately notify their Engineers of the same.

Keep sharp watch for obstructions, signals, trains breaking in two, etc.

Keep engines clean.

253. Firemen will be required to clean the engine jacket, hand-railing, domes, sand box, bell, cab, cylinder and steam-chest casings, smoke-stack and wood or coal space of tenders as often as necessary or required. Engineers will see that this is thoroughly done.

YARD WORK.

Clear passenger trains.

254. At all Yards where Yard Limit Signs are set and where the view is not obstructed, Yard Engines can work to within five (5) minutes of the time of a Passenger Train, and can occupy the main track on the time of a Passenger Train when they are officially notified of the number of minutes late, or the time the Passenger Train will arrive. When no Yard Limit Signs are set, Yard Engines will be governed by Rules 69 and 70.

Clear freight trains.

255. Yard Engines when working in Yards where Yard Limit Signs are set can occupy the main track until Freight Trains arrive, but should clear the main track as soon after their arrival as possible, and will be governed by Rule 104. If no Yard Limit Signs are set, observe particularly Rule 69. Yard Limit Signs should be set 2,500 feet beyond the extreme switch in either direction.

MISCELLANEOUS INSTRUCTIONS TO TRAIN MEN.

256. Every person in the Transportation Department, who is governed by the foregoing rules will secure a copy of same for which they must receipt. They are required to study them carefully, and be prepared to stand an examination at any time. Each person must pass a thorough examination before he can be permitted to dispatch, run a train or engine, or act as operator, or perform any of the duties above defined.

Secure copy of Rules and prepare for examination.

257. In case of an extraordinary rain storm at any point on the road, no train must pass over bridges, trestles or culverts until the train has first come to a full stop, and a man has been sent forward to make a thorough examination of the bridge, trestle or culvert.

Examine bridge and trestle after rain storms.

258. Concerning signals placed upon the Track while repairs are being made on Bridges or Track. Conductors and Engineers must observe the signals placed by Bridgemen or Trackmen. Every case of non-observance of such signals must be reported to the Superintendent of the Division, by telegraph, giving number of train and engine. See Rule 32.

Observe bridge and track signals.

259. Employes must avoid entering or passing through the sleeping cars, unless necessary, in the discharge of their duties. All unnecessary noise must be avoided about them at night, and care must be taken, in switching and handling, to disturb the inmates as little as possible.

Handle sleepers carefully—avoid passing through them.

260. Conductors, Agents, and others who are authorized to draw tools, material or supplies, are directed to practice the utmost economy in the use of the same. In making requisitions for lanterns, globes and such articles, a personal explanation will be required as to how they are broken or lost; and if broken or lost by carelessness, the Superintendent of the Division can

Economize in the use of tools and supplies.

require the guilty party to pay the cost price of the same.

261. No employe, whatever may be his rank, is allowed to take, for his own use, any Company supplies, material or other property, whether considered of value or otherwise. Every employe is expected to take such an interest in the welfare of the Company as will prevent persons from carrying off coal, wood, material and other property, and to discountenance all petty thieving, by promptly reporting the facts to the heads of their respective departments.

Must not appropriate Company's material.

Discountenance and report thieving.

CONCERNING HOT WATER HEATERS.

262. All steam heaters are fitted to burn anthracite coal of the "stove size," as lumps larger than a hen's egg will not feed well through the coils of worm. The safety lid should not be opened except to build the fire or put in coal.

Use anthracite coal. Keep safety lid closed.

263. The heater should be kept two-thirds full of coal at all times, and when an extra degree of heat is required the coal should not be allowed to get below the top of coil. This will give about sixteen inches of fire.

Keep heater two-thirds full of coal.

264. To increase or reduce the heat the dampers should be opened or closed, as may be required; and, by proper working of all the dampers and watching the indicators, the car can be kept at temperature desired.

Handle dampers properly.

265. Failure of heater may arise from neglect or from using an unsuitable grade of coal. Also from allowing fires to run too long without putting in coal, then filling them full and opening the

Why heaters fail.

draft, producing a rapid fire, which, instead of warming the car, stops the circulation, and is liable to create gases in the pipes.

266. Train Men should take extra care, in severe cold weather, to keep outside car doors closed as much as possible while trains are at stations, to prevent chilling of pipes.

Keep car doors closed.

267. When Train Men or Porters find any failure in the heater from want of circulation or blowing off at safety valve on top of drum, combination cocks leaking at end of drum, or frozen pipes, or any other defects, they will at once notify the nearest repair station by telegraph, and reduce the fire, so as not to burn the coil.

Telegraph any failure of the heaters.

268. In no case must the steam heaters be fired up when there is no water in pipes. The condition of which can be ascertained by looking at the inspection card in a rack near heater, provided for [illegible]urpose.

Do not fire up without water in pipes.

26[illegible] P[illegible]er cars having steam heaters shoul[illegible]ere weather, be turned so that heater [illegible] in forward end of car. This assists the circulation in pipes, and of hot air from the heater.

Turn cars with steam heaters during winter.

AGENTS.

270. Station Agents are responsible to and receive their instructions from the Superintendent of the Division, and will not absent themselves from their posts of duty without his consent.

To whom responsible. Must get permission to be absent.

271. They will comply strictly with all instructions given them by the Auditor, General Ticket Agent, and Car Accountant referring to matters pertaining to their departments.

Comply with instructions.

Care of Company's property.

272. Agents at Way Stations must go over their yards at least once every day and pick up all links, pins, grain-doors, or other property of a similar nature, and store the same in a secure place for future use.

Unnecessary assistants.

273. Agents who have authority to employ assistants, or laborers, are required to **keep their force cut down to conform to the amount of business done.** This they are expected to do without waiting for a special order from the Superintendent. Every Agent who fails in this respect neglects his duty.

Exercise courtesy.

274. Agents will see that their subordinates exercise courtesy in their dealings with the public and with each other.

Weighing cars.

275. In weighing cars they must in all cases be uncoupled at both ends and **stand** entirely alone and motionless upon the **scale. When** the weight of an empty car varies **200 pounds** from the weight marked on the car, **Agents will** telegraph at once to Division Superintendent, giving full particulars (number of car, number of train, weight marked on car, weight as shown by scales, etc.), to enable him to arrange with Superintendent of Machinery to have car remarked with correct weight at end of run.

Report irregularities.

Responsible for accidents to freight.

276. Station Agents will at once report, in writing, to their Division Superintendent all matters interfering with the interests of the Company or prompt dispatch of business, and all irregularities of conduct or neglect of duty on the part of employes. They will be held particularly responsible for accidents to freight or other property, occurring through deficient facilities that they have failed to report to their Superintendent.

277. They will not allow a car to stand upon the Main Track to be loaded or unloaded, without special permission from their Division Superintendent. Cars on main track.

278. Agents in flagging trains for passengers or freight, will display a white flag by day, and a white light by night. In flagging trains for other purposes, use green or red flags or lights, as per Rules 31 and 35. If, from any cause, Agents are required to use the white signals for other purpose than above described **they must swing the signals violently.** How to flag.

279. Station Agents are held responsible for the safety of switches, which must always (except when a man is standing by) be kept locked and right for trains running on the main track. (This is not intended to relieve Conductors and others from care of switches they may use; **whoever throws a switch upon side track must see it set back on main line.**) They must always see that the track is clear at stations, and, **in no case** allow a car to stand on the side track without the brake being properly applied to it, or the wheels securely blocked, and must personally examine the cars at their station before going home for the night, and when there are indications of a heavy wind. Station Agents and Conductors will see that cars are not allowed to stand on a siding at a point where the distance between the rails of the side track and main track is less than seven feet. Responsib for switches. Know that the main track is clear, and that cars on sidings are secured.

280. Ticket Agents must not sell tickets to points at which trains do not stop. Ticket sales.

281. Agents are required to notify their pas-

Passenger duties.

sengers when Passenger Trains are approaching, and if their duties do not require them to be in the ticket office while Passenger Trains are standing at their stations, they are expected to render all the assistance they can in loading baggage and aiding passengers. Agents must bear in mind that while a train, Passenger or Freight, is doing work at their stations, they must render all the assistance in their power to have the work done quickly and properly.

Aid in station work.

Report the refusal of local freight or cars.

282. Whenever a Conductor of a Local Freight Train refuses to take loose freight or cars offered to him, the Agent is required to report the fact to the Superintendent of the Division, giving name of Conductor and the reason assigned by him for not taking the freight or cars.

Avoid dispute.

283. Have no disputes with Conductors concerning switching or other work; notify trains what work you want done, and if they refuse, refer the matter to the Superintendent of the Division.

Boys climbing on cars and trains.

Hotel and bus runners.

284. They must use every effort to prevent boys climbing onto cars in the yard and jumping onto passing trains. They will not permit hotel and omnibus runners to ply their vocations upon the platforms or in the sitting rooms. It is an easy matter to have both the points covered by a city or village ordinance.

Baggage masters must wear badge.

285. Station Agents will see that the Station Baggage Master wears the regulation badge while on duty.

Be familiar with rules.

286. Station Agents are required to make themselves familiar with all the rules of the Company, and especially with those which in any way affect their duties.

CAR INSPECTORS.

287. Car Inspectors and others, whose duties require them to go under cars when in trains, must first position their **blue signal** and give notice to the Conductor and Engineer of their intention. At District and Division Terminals and other inspection stations, the Conductor of the train must see that the Inspector is clear of the train before giving signal to start. (See Rule 35½.)

Duty before going under cars.

CROSSING WATCHMEN.

288. Watchmen stationed at Street Crossings will be supplied with red and white flags and red and white lanterns. They must keep vigilant lookout for all **Trains** or **Engines,** and display the proper signals until they have passed. They must warn vehicles and pedestrians of the approach of trains or engines, and not permit crossing until it is safe to do so. They must stand where they can be seen by the Engineers of all trains, and must not depend upon the whistle for notice of approaching trains or engines. They will keep the lamps at crossings clean and lighted between Sunset and Sunrise and during foggy weather, and the rails at crossings flanged, and report all defects in the track or crossing planks to the Division Superintendent. Flagmen's houses are for the use of Watchmen, only, and must not be occupied by others.

REGULATIONS CONCERNING FREE PASSES.

Who may travel without passes.

289. The following Officers of this Railway and no others will be permitted to travel free without tickets or passes: The President, Vice Presidents, General and Assistant General Managers, Superintendent of Machinery, and Assistant Superintendent of Machinery; General Freight Agent; Superintendent Northern Pacific Express; General Ticket and Passenger Agent; Division Superintendents and Superintendent of Telegraph; Engineer in Chief and his principal Assistants; The General Solicitors and Land Commissioners; Superintendent and Engineer of Track, Bridges and Buildings. On their respective Divisions or Districts the following persons may travel free without passes: Assistant Superintendents, Train Dispatchers, Master Mechanics, Supervisors of Bridges and Buildings, Roadmasters.

Who may issue asses.

290. The passes of the following officers will be respected: The President; the Vice Presidents; the General and Assistant General Managers. Division Superintendents may pass employes of the Company within their respective Divisions.

No right to travel free.

291. The fact of being employed in the service of the Northern Pacific Railway Company, or of any other company, gives no right to travel free on any train. Persons entitled to travel free will be furnished with passes by the proper officers.

Must be written and signed in ink.

292. Passes must always be written and signed with ink, and must be on the blank forms provided for the purpose, when they can be obtained. Passes written or signed with lead pencil will not be honored by Conductors.

Trip passes.

293. Trip passes will be given for passage only in one direction, and not for **return.**

Look to the signatures on passes.

294. The signature and countersignature of a pass must invariably be written by the proper person, and Conductors are directed to refuse a pass signed or countersigned with the name of any officer "by" any person.

Telegraph passes.

295. Passes by telegraph will only be given by the President, Vice President and General Manager, Assistant General Managers, and Engineer in Chief, except for employes, as further provided in this rule—Such passes will only be given in the following form:

To Conductor, Train No. ......

Form of telegraph pass.

This telegram, countersigned by the Agent and stamped with the office stamp, will pass............. ....from........................Station to ....Station, on account of ....

Signed...................... ......

Superintendents can send telegraph passes to employes of their Division. Conductors will send all telegraph passes taken up by them to the Auditor with their daily reports, and they will refuse all that do not strictly conform to these directions.

Pass on freight rains.

296. Conductors of Freight Trains are strictly prohibited from allowing any person, whatever, to travel in the Caboose Cars or elsewhere on their train without special pernfits to do so, excepting persons holding Employes' Passes, and the officers named in Rule 290. This rule may be suspended as to a particular train on any part of the line, by notation on the Time Table, such suspension remaining in force only during the continuance of that Time Table.

Who may ride in mail, express and baggage cars.

297. Conductors must always examine the Express and Mail Rooms, and not permit anyone to ride in them, except the regular Express and Mail Agents on duty. They will not permit anyone in the Baggage Car except the Baggageman, and they will not permit any News Agent or Newsboy whatever to ride on their train without a pass.

Permits to ride on engine.

298. Permits to ride on the engine may be given by the Manager and Assistant General Managers, Superintendent of Machinery and Division Superintendents; but such permits must in every case be taken up by the Conductors and returned with their train reports.

Passes hold good.

299. Annual Passes issued by this Company are good until January 15th, following the year for which issued. All trip passes expire with the year.

NORTHERN PACIFIC BENEFICIAL ASSOCIATION.

RULES AND REGULATIONS

WITH INSTRUCTIONS TO FOREMEN AND OTHERS.

ASSESSMENTS.

1. All officers and employes connected with the operating departments of the N. P. R. R. are required to become members, and are assessed for this fund, excepting: Those over forty-five years of age at the time of entering the Company's service; Employes on temporary duty; Employes whose monthly compensation is less than $25, with whom membership is voluntary; Those afflicted with chronic diseases before entering the service of the Company. Membership. Exceptions.

2. The assessments are deducted monthly on the pay roll. Assessments on pay roll.

3. The monthly rate of compensation shall be the basis in determining the amount of the assessment. Basis of assessment. How determined.

When employes are paid by a monthly salary, the assessment shall be in accordance with the monthly rate of salary. Monthly salary.

When men are employed on daily wages, the monthly rate is to be computed by multiplying the daily pay by 26, this number being assumed to Monthly wages.

represent the number of working days in a calendar month. When the gross earnings of men thus employed in any one month exceed $100, by reason of overtime or overwork, they shall be assessed in proportion to their earnings for that month, in accordance with the general provisions of Article 4, Constitution.

Ten hours shall be considered a day's work for men who are paid by the hour.

Assessed each month in proportion to earnings for that month.

Locomotive engineers who receive a compensation based upon the number of miles run, shall pay an assessment each month as determined by the amount of their earnings for that month, in accordance with the provisions of Article 4 of the Constitution, defining the dues of members.

Assessment due from any earnings for fractions of a month.

4. The assessment, determined by the monthly rate of compensation, in accordance with the regulations of Rule 3, shall be deducted from any sum due by reason of services for fractional parts of a month.

No fractional assessment.

5. The assessment, whenever deducted, shall be the full sum properly chargeable, no fraction thereof.

EXEMPTIONS.

Temporary employes.

6. Employes on temporary duty, or on service which is presumed and intended to be of temporary duration only for a limited time, and who are to be discharged at the close of that service, shall not be liable to any assessment. It is intended that the obligations and benefits of the Association are to apply only to such as are considered regular employes of the Railroad Company. Parties making up pay rolls should indicate in the column for deductions that such employes are temporary.

7. Employes who work in two or more places on the railroad during any one month, shall be liable to but *one* assessment for that month. The deduction should be charged on the pay roll covering services first rendered. The assessment must be deducted in all cases, however, unless satisfactory evidence is presented showing that a deduction has been made for the same month on another pay roll.

One assessment for each month.

8. Where exemptions from assessments are properly made, the reason thereof should be briefly stated on the pay roll; otherwise the omission would be liable to correction by the Auditor.

State exemptions on pay roll.

9. Employes exempt by reason of age should be marked "over age" on the pay roll in column for deductions.

Over age.

10. Employes belonging to the exempt classes, who may be improperly assessed, will not thereby be entitled to claim benefits.

Assessments improperly made cannot claim benefits.

11. Where no assessments have been paid, there can be no claim for benefits, based simply on service to the Railroad Company, and such employes are not entitled to any medical services at the expense of the Beneficial Association or Railroad.

No assessment, no benefits.

AGE LIMITATION.

12. The limitation of age, established in Article 3. Section 2, By-Laws, requires that present employes of the Railroad shall not exceed fifty years at *the time of the commencement of the Association*, and that *new* employes of the Railroad shall not be received as members when over forty-five years of age. This limitation applies, how-

Limitation of age.

ever, only to the beginning of their membership. Having once been received, and the assessment properly commenced, their assessment and privileges will continue, irrespective of age, so long as they remain in the service of the Railroad.

MEDICAL SERVICE.

Invalids not to be employed.

Duties of foreman.

Physical examination.

13. Since the Association assumes, under prescribed limitations, the medical care of all employes who are assessed, whilst in the service of the Company, foremen and others whose duties require them to employ hands, should make inquiry as to the physical condition and state of health of all applicants for employment, and where these are manifestly unsound their services should preferably be declined. Where a reasonable doubt exists, the applicant should be sent to an authorized surgeon for examination.

Surgeon's order.

14. In order to obtain medical service from any authorized surgeon, the "Surgeon's Order"—Form 100—from the immediate superior officer, or head of department, must be furnished.

Discharge certificates.

From Sanitarium.

15. All patients treated in the Sanitarium are furnished on leaving with a Discharge Certificate, Form 113. When this certificate is printed in **red**, the person named may be re-employed; when printed in **black** it signifies that it will be for the interest of the service that the person named therein should **not** be re-employed.

From Line Surgeons.

16. Discharge Certificate, Form 103, will be furnished to all patients, whether treated by the line surgeons or at the Sanitarium. This discharge is to be endorsed by the foreman, and in all cases forwarded to the Surgeon of Sanitarium at Brainerd, after being thus endorsed.

CLAIMS AND ALLOWANCES.

17. An allowance will be made, in accordance with the published regulations, for time lost by reason of total disability when resulting from injuries or sickness, *providing ordinary pay is suspended* during such disability.

Time allowance.

18. When disability occurs by reason of accident or illness, and it be the intention to apply for allowance to which contributors are entitled, a claim must be filed with the Secretary upon Form 3 for accident, or Form 4 for illness.

Claim must be filed on proper blanks.

19. Application for death claim, when death results from accident, shall be made on Form 8.

Death claims.

Application for death claim, when death results from sickness, shall be made on Form 18.

20. On receipt of claim, where no objection exists after examination thereof, the application will be duly approved and voucher issued at appointed date for amount due.

Approval.

When paid.

21. No claims can be paid or allowances made unless an application has been filed in proper form.

No allowances unless claim has been filed.

22. Division Superintendents, when sending bills for settlement covering death and burial expenses, shall always forward with such bills a certificate of membership and death, on Form 16 where death results from accident, or on Form 17 where death results from sickness. It is to be clearly understood that any amount paid for such claims shall be credited to and deducted from any death claims that may be made subsequently under the provisions of Article 2, Sections 3 and 5, By-Laws.

Burial expenses.

EXCEPTIONS TO BENEFITS.

Injuries where no benefits.

23. The benefits of the Association will not be extended to cases of accident or personal injury caused by improper or unlawful acts of the claimant.

Sickness where no benefits.

24. Sickness resulting from intemperance, from evil habits, from improper conduct, from unlawful acts, cases of chronic disease contracted prior to entering the service, or venereal complaints, will not be treated at the expense of the Association.

No benefits in cases named.

25. *No contributor will be entitled to claim benefits when disability arises from these causes.*

Violation of orders.

26. Accidents or sickness resulting from a violation of orders will not entitle contributor to benefits.

Cases that are not received at hospital.

27. Chronic complaints contracted prior to entering the service of the Northern Pacific Railroad Company, contagious or venereal diseases, will not be received for treatment at the hospital.

Hospital patients have no time allowance.

28. Patients treated as inmates of the Sanitarium, Brainerd, do not receive the time allowance.

MISCELLANEOUS INSTRUCTIONS.

State names correctly.

29. Special care should be observed by heads of departments and foremen to state the names of employes *correctly* when filling the certificates required in applications for benefits. Errors in this lead to difficulties in making payments and taking receipts.

Constitution and By-laws.

Summary.

30. The Secretary will furnish, upon application, a copy of the Constitution and By-Laws, and also of the "Summary," the latter containing a brief statement of the benefits and methods of the Association.

31. Proper forms or blanks can be obtained by application to Division Superintendents, to Master Mechanics, or to the Secretary. Blanks, where had.

32. Applications for all claims and allowances must be made upon the proper blanks, and forwarded to H. W. Knauff, Secretary N. P. B. A., St. Paul. When approved, payment of the amount due will be made by voucher. **No payment of any of these claims will be made through the Paymasters.** Claims, where sent. Paid by voucher.

INSTRUCTIONS FOR THE CARE OF INJURED PERSONS.

It often becomes a duty to administer to the sufferings of those who meet with accidents on the line of the Road, as hours must elapse, frequently, before surgical aid can be reached; since much of the country through which the Road passes is sparsely settled. It is in these cases of emergency that great service may be rendered to the wounded in relieving them of pain, in preventing permanent disablement, and perhaps even in saving life. In order to accomplish these ends, the following instructions are appended, substantially the same as those prepared by Dr. John W. Trader for the employes of the M., K. & T. R. R., and by Dr. Bancroft of the Denver & Rio Grande R. R.; and a small box containing a few medicines, bandages, etc., is entrusted to the care of Train Conductors. Aid in emergencies.

If these instructions are not fully understood, or if additional information is desired in reference Instructions.

to the temporary management of cases that may come under care, an explanation of the simpler methods of attending to injuries may be had by application to the Surgeon at the N. P. Sanitarium, Brainerd, or to any of the authorized medical officers of the Company.

MEDICINAL CONTENTS OF CHEST.

Medicines.

No. 1. Laudanum.—Give fifteen or twenty drops every two or three hours, to relieve pain. If pain be severe, give it every hour, but not for more than *four* hours in succession. Stop its use when pain is relieved.

No. 2. Ammonia Mixture.—Give a half-teaspoonful in water every hour, after any severe injury, or in fainting from hemorrhage or other cause.

INJURIES OF THE HEAD.

Bruises of head.

In simple bruises of the head, when the skin is not cut through to the bone, apply a compress and bandage, keeping the dressing wet with water.

Concussion of brain.

In concussion of the brain the patient is either insensible or delirious. Keep the head cool, the feet warm, and give a half-teaspoonful in water of mixture No. 2.

Injuries of head.

In severe injuries of the head, as fractures, slightly elevate the head, unfasten the clothes about the throat and waist, and keep the patient quiet. If there is bleeding from the nose or mouth, use cold applications to head and face, and turn the patient on his side, so that the blood can run out of the mouth. Also, keep the feet warm.

INJURIES TO THE CHEST.

When one or more ribs are broken, seat the patient in the chair, with his arms around the neck of an assistant, who will lift up until the patient's body is on a stretch, then apply the wide bandage, taking four or five turns, pin snugly, then lay the patient flat on his back.

Broken ribs.

FRACTURES.

When the collar bone is broken, tie the shoulder back by bandages passed under the arm and over the back, like a figure eight, 8, then put the arm in a sling, slightly elevating the elbow.

Broken collar bone.

When the long bones are broken, as arms or legs, pull the limbs as nearly as possible into proper shape, observing this rule: When the broken bone is bent towards a right angle, and shortened, extend by pulling in direction of the angle until the ends of the bone approach each other, then straighten the limb. When the ends of bones have been thrust through the muscles, you must first release them from this unnatural and painful position before attempting to straighten them. The following diagram will illustrate:

Broken arms

Broken legs.

Fractured bone entangled in the muscle.

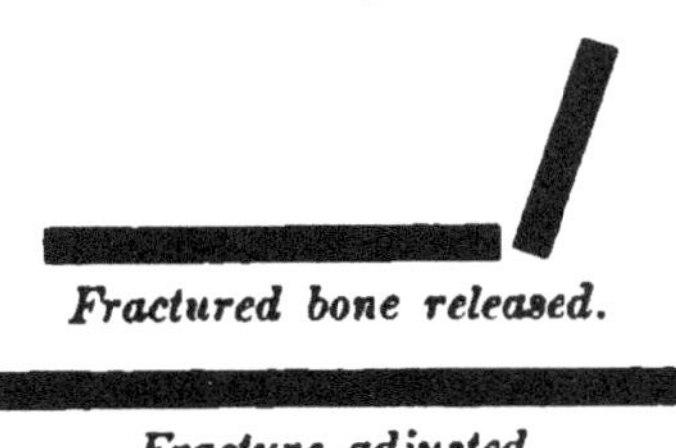

Fractured bone released.

Fracture adjusted.

When a fractured limb is reduced and placed in something like its natural position, there should be very little pain; neither should there be much pain in reducing a fracture if the proper care and gentleness be observed. Fractures should be adjusted as soon after the injury as possible. After you have straightened the limb out parallel with the body, make it fast—if a leg, to its fellow; if an arm, the bandage should encircle the body. Fracture should be firmly held by the bandage, so as to avoid too much motion in the broken bone, but care must be taken not to bind unevenly and too tightly.

In case the patient is not to be moved, there is no necessity for binding the limb, but allow it to lie in the most comfortable position, covering it with cloths wrung out of warm water.

DISLOCATION.

Dislocations.

Many, and nearly all, of the dislocations can be reduced by attending to them immediately. The fingers, wrist and elbow joints, by gently pulling on them, and at the same time, pressing them into place. The shoulder, when knocked down, is easily reduced by grasping the dislocated arm and elevating it over the patient's head, then let some one place both thumbs under the joint in the armpit and press up firmly, while the arm is brought gently but firmly down until it is parallel with the body; then put the arm in a sling, slightly elevating the elbow.

CRUSHED AND BRUISED LIMBS.

By far the greater number of railroad injuries are of this class. Fortunately, there is very little danger of severe bleeding. The treatment is to immerse the injured limb in milk-warm water, or envelop it with cloths wrung out of warm water. Do not bind a crushed hand or foot. Sometimes the pain is very intense when the system awakens from the shock. In this case, give fifteen or twenty drops of laudanum, as already directed.

Crushed and bruised limbs.

BLEEDING WOUNDS.

Bleeding in wounds may be stopped, ordinarily, by binding a compress over them which has previously been dipped in cold water. Should the wound, however, be bleeding profusely (spurting blood), crowd into the wound some styptic wool, and then apply a bandage firmly over it. If this method fails, and it be a hand or an arm that is injured, place the bandage loosely above the elbow three or four inches; if it be a foot or a leg, place it four or five inches above the knee, but if the bleeding is in the upper arm or leg apply the bandage above the wound, after which observe this rule: Put a large cork or a hard roller bandage on the inside of the limb under the bandage; then place under it, immediately on top of the cork or roller, a small stick or lead pencil and twist steadily until the hemorrhage stops. Care should be exercised that this twist is not firmer than is required to arrest the bleeding, nor continue longer than is necessary to reach experienced help.

Bleeding, how arrested.

BURNS AND SCALDS.

Soft cloths, dipped in the white of eggs beaten up with sweet oil, may be applied to relieve pain;

or a solution of bi-carbonate of soda (baking soda, which can generally be found in every house), made by disolving three or four tablespoonfuls in one quart of water, may be applied in the same manner.

Burns and scalds.

Internally give laudanum (No. 1) to relieve pain, and if the burn is extensive, give also strong coffee and whisky and ammonia mixture (No. 2).

FROST-BITE.

Frostbites.

Remove the person frozen to a cold room and immerse the frozen parts in ice water, or carefully rub them with snow. Care should be taken not to scratch nor break the skin. From one-half hour to three hours should be spent in removing the frost from the affected parts. After the frost has been expelled, the patient should be removed to a comfortable room, the limb elevated and lightly covered, and cooling lotions applied. If vesicles appear, equal parts of lime water and sweet oil may be applied.

RUPTURE.

Ruptures.

Sometimes after a severe strain a tumor suddenly appears in the groin, and not unfrequently extends into the scrotum. Whenever this occurs place the patient on his back in a recumbent position, with the limbs flexed; then place the hand on the tumor, and press gently obliquely upward and outwards. When it is reduced, keep it in position until you find a surgeon. When, however, it is not easily returned, do not use violence, but make applications of cold water until the services of a surgeon can be obtained.

NOTIFY SURGEON.

Whenever an accident occurs on the line, the Conductor must immediately telegraph the Surgeon in whose charge the injured person is to be placed, in order that time may be given to prepare for reception of the patient.

Notify surgeon at once.

TRAMPS INJURED.

In cases of injury inflicted by trains upon intoxicated persons on the track, tramps stealing rides, etc., where the employes of the Road are in no way to blame, the injured persons must, of course, be carried to a station where humane and proper treatment can be bestowed; but, as such persons are generally without means, it is not advisable to take them out of the county in which the accident occurs. All such cases should be placed under the care of the county authorities where the injury occurred, as early as possible. In no instance are they to be removed beyond the limits of such county without express orders to that effect from the Division Superintendent; for, if removed beyond the county limits, the Railroad Company may be held responsible for treatment and support.

Injuries to tramps.

Not to be removed from county.

USE OF LIQUOR.

The continued, or the excessive periodical use of malt or alcoholic liquors should be abstained from by every one engaged in operating the road, not only on account of the great risks to life and property incurred by intrusting them to the oversight of those whose intellects may be dulled at

Avoid use of liquors.

times when most care is needed, but also, and especially, because *habitual drinking has a very bad effect upon the constitution*, which is a serious matter for men so liable to injury as railroad employes always are. It so lessens the recuperative powers of the body that simple wounds are followed by the most serious and dangerous complications. Fractures unite slowly, if at all, and wounds of a grave nature, such as those requiring the loss of a limb, are almost sure to end fatally. NO EMPLOYE CAN AFFORD TO TAKE SUCH RISKS, AND THE RAILWAY COMPANY CANNOT ASSUME SUCH RESPONSIBILITIES.

Injurious results.

INDEX.

INDEX.

INDEX.

www.ingramcontent.com/pod-product-compliance
Lightning Source LLC
Chambersburg PA
CBHW030538270326
41927CB00008B/1426
* 9 7 8 3 7 4 4 7 2 7 9 3 8 *